MEAN
TIME
LOVE

A WOMAN'S JOURNEY FROM
SELF-LOATHE TO SELF-LOVE

Anita Ross

Published in the United States by: Anita Ross

Printed in the United States of America

**For information about special discounts on bulk purchases, please send
inquiries to:** info@anitaross.net

Designed by: Juan Millan of Creave, Inc.

Edited by: Maria Pelaez

Library of Congress Control Number: 2011901565

ISBN: 978-0-61544-089-7

1st Edition, March 2011

*It is Anita Ross' mission to empower millions of women to love themselves fully and to
equip them with the tools to do so. To find out more about booking Anita for speaking
engagements or workshops, please visit us at: www.anitaross.net.*

This book is dedicated to my husband,
BFF and partner in "difference making"…
Kevin, thank you for loving me the way you do
and for inspiring me to walk my talk.
I choose you.

FOREWORD

I once heard that "a woman's heart is an ocean of many secrets." If this is true, then the book that you are about to read will not only take you deep into the ocean of a lion-hearted woman, but also reveal the secrets that are found at the bottom.

If you are a woman who has been walking down that dark tunnel of self despair, depression, confusion, abuse, loneliness, sadness, hopelessness, and fear, then this book is the light at the end of the tunnel. On the other side of the tunnel of your pain and fear, you will meet Anita Ross standing there with a light of hope and inspiration and an exit sign, pointing you to a life of self-love and confidence.

She can do so not because she graduated at the top of her class from a prestigious university with a Master's in engineering, or because she's led a 10 year career working for Fortune 500's in corporate America, or because she is the Executive Director of a not for profit that she co-founded. She can introduce you to the path because at the same time as she had every worldly success, she was also living every woman's nightmare of abuse, low self-esteem, and one toxic relationship after another. In this book, Anita shares the nuggets produced by her soul that gave her the power to bounce back and to overcome every imaginable adversity. She shows you what every woman needs to know about themselves that always opens the door to pain, disappointment, and even depression. She also gives you the key to staying balanced even in the face of the most turbulent storms. Her research is her life. Her classroom is her relationships. Her thesis is this book. Her diploma is you living a life, where you and millions of women learn to love yourselves fully.

As her husband, I only wish I could have met her sooner. However, if I had, perhaps, you would not have this rich well to drink from. Learn from the powerful encounters, fine distinctions, and the incredible journey from my greatest teacher. Let her show you, as she shows me everyday – a deeper kind of love.

Kevin Kitrell Ross
January 2, 2011
Sacramento, California

CONTENTS

PREFACE

I wrote this book because *one woman in the world feeling unlovable is one too many!* Feeling unlovable equates to not loving yourself, not feeling worthy of love and not extending love to others. Time is of the essence! Each day that a woman makes choices without loving herself is a day that she will make harmful choices. It is a day she may be abused by her partner. It is a day she may neglect herself. It is a day she may withhold love from her child. It is a day she may suppress her dream. It is a day she may starve herself. It is a day she may overeat. It is a day she may do drugs. It is a day she may cut herself. It is a day she may attempt suicide. If this book can help at least one woman avoid a day like this then I have done my job. *Ultimately, I aim for a world where all women are bursting with love that outpours on to and into others and rids our society of the many ills plaguing it.*

This book is for the woman who wants to love herself or learn how to love herself more. It's for the woman in a relationship that she knows isn't good for her. It's for the woman looking for unconditional and lasting love. It's for the woman who spends more time taking care of others than herself. It's for the woman looking for a sense of control over her life. It's for the woman who spends more money on clothes than she can afford. It's for the woman looking to take her career to the next level. It's for the woman who eats too much or who does not eat enough. It's for the woman who is too busy to spend a moment alone. It's for the woman who has an addiction she can't quite conquer—or who loves someone who does. It's for the woman struggling to have her voice heard. It's for the woman who feels like she is on a roller coaster each day of her life. It's for the woman who is finding her way. It's for the woman that wonders why nothing can go right for her. It's for the woman that is searching for a way out of the mess she calls her life. It's for the woman seeking understanding about her life. It's for the woman who wants to learn more about herself. If you can identify with one or more of these scenarios, please remember that you are not alone.

People often ask me why this book is directed to women when there is a wealth of information here that men can benefit from. John Gray, author of *Men are From Mars, Women are from Venus* says his "Work is constantly striving towards not proving that one is superior to the other, but that we are different. We all have our unique vulnerabilities and we have predispositions towards certain behaviors." This is exactly my premise. While I encourage everyone to read this book, I also acknowledge that there are definite differences between men and women. According to the American Journal of Psychiatry, women inherit depression more often than men and women are more likely to stay in abusive relationships. Another study by the American Journal of Psychiatry shows that 12-step programs such as Alcoholics Anonymous (AA) are not as effective for women as they are for men. The AA process begins with "We admit we are powerless over alcohol and that our lives have become unmanageable." The study goes on to say that "Many women already feel powerless. Despite gains that women have made in recent years, they still live in a world dominated by men." This causes a resistance that some women cannot get beyond. "One out of every six women has been the victim of an attempted or completed rape in her lifetime as opposed to one out of every thirty-three men."[1] These are just a few examples of how women and men differ. It just so happens that my life path has led me to having a keen understanding of women and knowing how to help them break through self-esteem issues, adversity, circumstances and limiting beliefs so that they see the limitless possibilities for themselves. So if you are in relationship with women, whether it's yourself, your mother, sister, relative, lover or friend, I invite you to read on. There is value here for you.

Disclosure: Please be advised that in order to protect the identity of any persons mentioned in this book, actual names and details have not been used.

ACKNOWLEDGMENTS

I thank my exquisite, extraordinary, inspiring, angels of love, Angelina and Kameela for showing me that my capacity to love is times infinity. I didn't know I could love so hard. You make me a better person and this world a better place. I love you both bigger than the world!

I thank my mother and father for loving me unconditionally and always making it loud and clear. You have taught me how to take a stand for what I believe in and to have the confidence to do so. As the Celine Dion song says "I'm everything I am, because you loved me."

I thank my sister for loving me through the rough patches and being the difference when it really counts. Thank you for bearing with me all these years so that we could get to the "good stuff" of being sisters. I love that we know each other like no other can.

I thank my Grandma Carmen and Grandpa Seymour for teaching me so many lessons about life, love, wisdom and joy.

I thank my Grandma Iris and Grandpa Roque for the love, laughter and memories that will always make me smile.

I thank my aunts and uncles, Roque, Robin, Donna, Norma, Ray and Ellie for the unending support you give me from milestone to milestone and from near or far. I hope you feel my love as strongly as I feel yours.

I thank my Uncle David for holding me in your heart, and for having a special place in mine, always!

I thank my 'Cousins Night Out Crew Plus Three', Aixa, Tina, Edgardo, Gabriel, Chakshu, Michael, Roberto, Steve, Margo, Anna, Damien and Cameron, for showing me that family does not just mean the exchange of love but it is also that of friendship. I love the bond we have collectively and the individual bonds I have with each of you.

I thank Maria Pelaez for…oh gosh there really aren't words that can truly express who you are for me but I will try…thank you for being my best friend, my fellow "foodie", my coach, my confidante, my advocate, my editor, my proofreader and for giving of your talents to the development of this book. Your candor, heart and skills took this book to the next level. You are a marvelous person and I am grateful you choose me as a friend.

I thank Misty Hubbard for loving me like we've been friends for a lifetime. Thank you for always having the right and perfect words that uplift and inspire me to be the best woman that I can be.

I thank Andrea Doakes for believing in me, supporting my work and being a phenomenal friend. You teach me what friendship looks like when you are willing to do whatever it takes to honor it. I love you and your apple cream pie.

I thank Freda Shadlow for creating the most amazing environment for my daughters to grow up in while I was out writing this book. I love how you love my daughters and how they love you. The smile on their faces when they see you or say "Mimi" is priceless. This book exists because of you.

I thank Maxine Groves for lending her tremendous heart, keen knowledge and unparalleled wisdom to this book. It is an honor to have you in my life. I love you.

I thank Reverend Chris Michaels for lending his heart, mind, time and class to this book. You communicate in a way that reaches my soul. You are a great friend and mentor.

I thank Eve Hogan for her developmental editing talents that had me stretch my vision for this book. Thank you for the fearless feedback.

I thank Juan Millan of Creave, Inc. for catching the vision of this book and creating the best book cover and layout a girl could ask for. You have a lifetime customer in me.

I thank Kaylee Sheddrick and the Unity Village Bookstore staff for keeping a spot warm for the pregnant lady to write in the middle of a Missouri Winter and making sure I had the best decaf lattes in town.

I thank Tiffany Golden for taking care of my daughters as I took this book into the homestretch. Thank you for loving them and being the best Sec of Defense the Ross' could ask for. We love you.

I thank all of the women who have participated in my A Deeper Kind of Love workshops for being my inspiration, for trusting me and allowing me to be a part of their journey.

I thank everyone who has supported me in the process of creating this book. I have realized one of my BIG dreams because of you.

I thank Margaux Rooney for furthering my mission by bringing my work to WEAVE, Inc. Your genuine care for domestic violence and sexual abuse survivors is changing lives.

I thank my Teen Dream Camp volunteers and supporters for giving tirelessly to our cause. Together we have deeply impacted so many lives and will continue to do so because of you!

I thank Crystal Garcia for being the wind beneath my wings. Teen Dream Camp is, because of you. You are so amazing!

I thank Karina Iglesias for bringing positive, uplifting and soulful music into the world. You are a superstar on stage and in my life.

I thank God for embracing and loving me as I am. Thank you for the journey.

INTRODUCTION

"Life as a mother
It's hard for me to sit back and see
The same thing that happened to me
Happen to you.
This ain't love.
But here's the love
I want to give to you"
- Good Woman Down, A song by Mary J. Blige

I was new in the area. I had just finished my freshman year in college and had landed a highly coveted summer internship with the United States Patent Office in Crystal City, Virginia. I was living with five other women in a wonderful apartment overlooking a park in a great part of town in Washington D.C. I enjoyed the city. I took walks often, visited Georgetown on a regular basis, made new friends everyday and enjoyed high profile events that the internship had to offer at various places on Capitol Hill. At my office, my role was Patent Examiner in the Water Purification unit. I had a great supervisor who was very impressed with my sharp analytical mind and keen ability to find improved ways of doing things.

One day on my walk to the Metro, a man in a very nice car pulled over and got out to let me know that he could not help but come over to tell me how beautiful I was and that he would be remiss if he did not ask if he could take me out sometime. While it was not particularly unusual for a man to approach me in such a way, this time something caught my attention. I was impressed with his looks, the way he was dressed and his car. After a bit more chit chat, we exchanged numbers and I went about the rest of my day. Later that evening he called me. We had a great conversation and by the end of the call, I agreed to go out with him the next night. I figured, why not? I loved to dine out and he was a good looking, respectable man.

Our date was fabulous. Tony was a really smooth guy. Everywhere we went he knew people and we got the royal treatment. I felt like he went out of his way to make me feel special.

A couple of days later it was the weekend and Tony invited me out for some sightseeing. It sounded great and I immediately said yes. I got dolled up in a cute summer dress and a hot pair of sandals. We had a great day. I saw amazing monuments, walked along the Potomac River and I really enjoyed the little city of Bethesda. It was late in the day when he asked me if we could stop by his house really quickly. He just needed to pick something up and we were only about a mile away. When we arrived, he asked if I would like to see where he lived. I was curious but something in me told me to wait in the car, which I did.

Over the next week, we went out every night. I was having the time of my life and I was on cloud nine. I had no idea how good I could feel with a guy that I had only known for two weeks. Admittedly, my relationships up to that point were nothing to brag about. Almost all of them were with guys that were not up to much in their lives, hung out on the streets all the time and had no clue how to treat a lady. But all of my friends were dating the same type of guys and so it just seemed to be the way things were in my neighborhood. Tony was different. He had a great job, lots of money, knew about the finer things in life and most definitely knew how to treat me: from opening my car door to allowing me to order first at a restaurant to showing me new things. When the weekend hit, he asked me to come over to his house for a BBQ with some friends. Although I had known him only a short time, I trusted him and decided to go to his house because it sounded like fun. I left so excited that I forgot to tell my roommates where I was going. As a matter of fact, up to this point they did not even know about Tony.

As he held the car door open for me, he remarked on how sexy I looked. I smiled and felt good. When we arrived at his house, he took me to the basement. Turned out he did not own the house but was simply renting the basement. He explained that he was in transition and trying to figure out if he wanted to buy a house or rent an apartment so his friends offered this space while he made up his mind. While this was news to me, I also realized that there was no one else in the house and no BBQ grill outside of the patio doors. I turned around to ask him about the grill when I felt him grab me and push me against the wall. He began to kiss me forcefully and I could not get any words out. I wanted him to stop. When he stopped pressing his lips against me, he still had my arms pinned against the wall. I asked him to let me go and he said to me "I love you and I am so attracted to you, I can't control myself." I was scared but I remained calm. I asked him again to let go of my arms and rather than do so he took his legs and positioned them to ensure I could not move my legs very much. Now I moved from scared to angry.

I was trying my best to break loose but I could not. He kept repeating over and over how much he was in love with me and that he wanted to make love to me. He also kept pressing hard on my lips as if he was not interested in what I had to say in return. I kept trying to tell him I was not ready for that step but it was as if his ears were shut off. Finally, I begged him to let me go. I looked in his eyes and instead of seeing a controlling, violent man that would do such a thing to a woman, I saw his puppy dog eyes and for a moment I felt bad for him.

Suddenly he grabbed hold of me and threw me on his bed, which was only a few steps from where he held me against the wall. I could not believe what was happening. I no longer felt sorry for him. He pressed himself hard onto me. Tony was easily six and a half feet tall and extremely muscular. Compared to my five foot three inch frame and 110 pounds, there was nothing I could do in that moment to get him off me. He kept trying to convince me that I wanted to make love to him in between the hard kisses he kept forcing on me. I assured him that I did not and after about thirty minutes of this taunting, he finally decided to get his way. He forced himself on me and at some point during the rape, I gave in and stopped fighting. In order to get through this I needed to concentrate on the good things. So I repeated over and over silently to myself "he loves me, he loves me, he loves me…"

After he was finished, he asked me what I wanted to do next. I meagerly replied, I just want to go home and rest. On the drive home, he talked about how wonderful it was to finally make love to me. He also shared he felt that I was 'marriage material.' I heard him but was not listening. I just hoped that each traffic light we approached would be green so that the ride home would be as short as possible.

When I got home, three of my roommates were there eating pizza and recapping their days. They asked me to join them and

I did. The last thing I wanted in that moment was to be alone. I ate a slice of pizza and joined in the conversation as if everything were normal. They asked me where I had been for the past few weeks. Too ashamed to tell them what happened, I told them about this great guy I was dating and spending all my time with.

I went to bed in complete denial about being raped. I began to reexamine the situation and in an effort to make myself feel better, I started to make myself believe that I consented to having sex. That I was okay with it and it really wasn't so bad. Despite all the hurt and pain I was feeling, it was easier for me to think that I simply was not raped. I decided that if I was in a relationship with Tony it would all go away.

The next day I went on a date with him and continued to do so for the remainder of my summer internship.

When I returned to school, I found it easy to break it off with him and while he gave me a lot of grief about it, there was not much he could do from so far away. I didn't really care how he felt. I was eager to start a new semester and put Tony behind me.

It was not until two years later, when I found myself in an emotionally abusive relationship that I finally broke down. I was alone in my dorm room when I found myself crying uncontrollably. I was trying to pinpoint why I was crying so hard and what kept coming up for me was the rape. When I finally told someone, I felt as if a huge boulder had been lifted off my shoulders. The person encouraged me to tell my boyfriend and when I was ready I did. He did not believe me nor did he show any signs of caring. It was then that I packed my secret back up and reengaged my impenetrable shield.

W omen are phenomenal beings. We are loving, yet relentless. We are powerful, yet vulnerable. We are compassionate, yet tough. We are joyful, yet pensive. We are honest, yet vacillating. We are open, yet private. We are confident, yet apprehensive. We are faithful, yet analytical. We are spontaneous, yet pragmatic. We are leaders, yet supporters. We are sexy, yet conservative. We are reliable, yet whimsical. We are responsible, yet carefree. I could go on but I believe you get the point. Women are dynamic beings comprised of any and all characteristics. However, it is the unique combination and expression of these characteristics by each woman as she goes through life that dictates how she shows up in the world. Outside influences can get in the way of women seeing and expressing their greatness and so I am inspired to support women in knowing the truth about themselves, which is: Women are perfect, whole and complete at all times and in every way. The secret is loving yourself, through it all!

Immediately after being raped, I was not aware of my perfection. Subconsciously, I thought I was raped because I deserved it. In other words, I was not worth anything better. It wasn't until later in life that I realized it was an experience that I went through to learn more about my perfection! It may seem ironic but it's true. Every experience that I have been through, many of which I will share in this book, were immaculately crafted for me so that I would live my divine purpose! This is true for *everyone's* life path.

No matter what we go through, whether seemingly good or bad, it is meant to teach us more about who we truly are. Our experiences allow us to become more familiar with our *authentic selves*. Have you ever gotten a pedicure? The first time I got one, I instantly became a believer in the pedicure! I learned that I enjoy being pampered and having pretty feet. As a result, from that point forward I chose to get pedicures on a regular basis. An example on the opposite end of the spectrum is a child that touches a hot stove for the first time. He touches the stove and burns his little hand. In that moment he processes that he does not like how it feels to be burned. He learns that it hurts and chooses not to do it again. This is precisely how we learn about ourselves! Only the situation and circumstances of the event change. Now let me warn you, it is not always easy to hold steadfast to this truth because life can throw us some real curveballs that can be hurtful, painful and often difficult to shake. It is my intention, through this book to share with you some distinctions, principles, tools and most importantly to inspire you to love yourself fully no matter what you have been through, are going through or what your future holds.

Over the course of my life, I have discovered that many women are drifting through life, consciously or unconsciously, believing they are not lovable. Thinking and feeling this way has the power to leave us susceptible to choosing people, experiences and things that do not serve our highest good and land us in circumstances that quickly seem out of our control.

Feeling unlovable stems from the idea that love is 'out there' somewhere waiting to be found. And due to many earthly influences, women have the notion that they must search externally for love. In fact, we grow up with a list of "musts" and "shoulds": we must get married, we must have children, we must be thin or we should act like a lady or we should be strong no matter what comes our way. It is exhausting to think that we must do and be all these things in order to find love! And when we don't meet these expectations we feel bad about it. We feel like a failure, incomplete, not enough, unworthy, less than, inferior, ugly, etc. The list of unlovable feelings goes on, simply pick your poison.

What we lose sight of is that the love we are searching for is right there within us. Everything that makes you lovable is already within you! You were born with it all and it will be with you eternally no matter what you learn from the daily happenings of life! Picture a newborn baby with her exquisite features, her inquisitive eyes, her fearless way of expressing what she wants and her instinctive way of giving and receiving love. You are that perfect right now! It's okay if you do not embrace this belief yet but please give me the opportunity to present my case. I believe you will agree with me when it's all said and done.

﹏A NOTE TO THE READER

Mean Time Love unfolds in an evolutionary manner. It begins by laying a foundation comprised of distinctions, principles and perspectives that will open up your consciousness and make you available for transformation. It progresses to providing evidence, tools and practical exercises that will empower you to discover your authenticity and love yourself like never before.

Each chapter takes you on a journey through the following three phases:

M E A N

In this section, you will read about the real life experiences that led me to discovering the concept I call your *mean*. Your *mean* is the place where you unceasingly love and express your authentic self regardless of your circumstances, your past or how others perceive you.

T I M E

Time is the gift of patience you give yourself to reflect, interpret and learn from your experiences. In this section, I share the insights I gained from reflecting on my own life and experiences.

L O V E

Self-love is the experience of unwaveringly affirming your worth and perfection such that there is nothing that can make you believe otherwise. I close each chapter by sharing the knowledge and wisdom that I used to get myself off a perilous self-esteem roller coaster and live my life from my *mean*.

I must warn you, the road to your mean can be an emotional one, but please know that I will be with you every step of the way.

Thank you in advance for taking a peek into my heart.

Now, let's begin.

Chapter 1

The Choice is Yours

"I never wanted half of you
Sharing you will just not do
Gotta be, one on one, or it won't be done
You said you wanted all of me
Why couldn't it be two not three"

- Half of You, A song by Brownstone

 M E A N

I was sitting in my college dorm room trying to figure out whether what Jason said to me was true. I kept playing it over in my head, "It's over between Nadine and I. From now on, it's only you and me." Normally I couldn't stand to hear her name, Nadine, but this time it felt great. Although Jason's facial features were not actually good-looking, I found him to be a very attractive man. He had a sexy accent and a chiseled body that looked like it was out of a magazine. But what I, and most women, found appealing about him was nothing you could touch or see. It was an air about him that suggested he was impenetrable. He was hard and showed no signs of weakness. I knew that he was trying to get out of a relationship, but he had assured me that it would only be temporary. Eight tumultuous months later, after many an argument and many sad love songs, he left Nadine. I was ecstatic. It was official, I was now his girlfriend. All that I had been fighting for was mine. But it was time to go to class, so I grabbed my books and headed out feeling triumphant.

Averaging a GPA of 3.5 in Engineering, tutoring various levels of calculus, working round the clock as a Residential Assistant and juggling various other jobs, was tiring for me. However, I was excelling in everything I did. Or so it seemed. It had been a rough day. I finally got back to my room and started searching for something to munch on when the phone rang. It was Jason. He asked me to come over and spend the night with him. I wanted to so I asked him when he would be by to pick me up. He explained that he didn't want to lose his great parking spot and told me to walk. Despite my state of fatigue, I packed my bag, grabbed my books and commenced my trek across campus.

It was dark outside and I was kind of spooked but I kept going. For an evening in the middle of a New York winter, I thought to myself that at least it wasn't as cold as it could've been. All of a sudden, I noticed three men walking in my direction. They appeared to be coming from the frat party that was just up the road from which I could hear the faint sounds of a Led Zeppelin song playing. Laughing hysterically and looking a little disheveled, I could tell they did not have a care in the world. They had gained on me quickly and were suddenly so close that I could smell the beer on their breath. When they focused on me, they started whistling and heckling. It was uncommonly nerveracking for me that night. I remained calm, avoided eye contact and kept moving, only at a faster pace. The air was intense. I took a deep breath and focused. I could hear the loudest one, with his grizzly uneven beard, uttering "Hola mami...dame un beso...let's go back to my room and do the cuchifrito", in his mocking Americanized accent. He grabbed me by the arm and pulled me towards him. I froze at the thought of what was next. Was I going to have to kick him? Should I scream? With all of these thoughts running through my head, he released his hold on me. My immediate reaction was to give them a piece of my mind but then I realized there was three of them and only one of me. I was powerless. All I could do is walk as fast as I could while tears of anger and sadness rolled down my cheeks. I finally reached my destination. It took a lifetime to get there.

Jason was sitting on the couch in the common area of his apartment. I had tried to gain my composure prior to arriving but as I stepped into the apartment, I burst into tears. Without getting up from the sofa, Jason asked me why I was crying. I could not pull myself together. All of my feelings of outrage and inadequacy had culminated into this uncontrollable display of emotion. Jason was becoming increasingly impatient. "You're crying like a big fat baby," he uttered. Irritated by the fact that I was incoherent in my attempts to answer his question, he abruptly told me to go in his bedroom and stop crying. He said that he would talk to me only after I calmed down.

It was going on 2:00 AM, and I had spent that last couple of hours anticipating his entrance into the room. I thought for sure he would come in to check on me and discuss what happened. It seemed like forever before Jason came in. He undressed without a word. Then he undressed me. We never mentioned the evening again.

A season had passed and it was the first summer I would spend on campus. I had landed an esteemed internship working in a research lab and while at it I figured I would take a summer class. I managed to get my own room with no roommate and Jason had just moved off campus into a house that he shared with one other person. It was somehow 'cooler' to have a boyfriend that lived off campus. Things were looking good. The routine quickly became class in the morning, work in the afternoon and usually Jason's house at night.

It was an odd week. I had only spent one night with Jason earlier in the week and was excited to go see him. When I got there Jason had dinner already prepared. I gobbled down my food and headed upstairs to the bedroom to watch some TV. Jason mentioned that he would be up after he cleaned the kitchen. I was tidying up the room since it was kind of a mess. Suddenly the phone rang and about fifteen minutes later he returned to tell me that I had to leave immediately because Nadine was on her way. I could not believe my ears. Did he actually say that I had to leave because his ex-girlfriend was on her way? And as if it was no big deal? As I paced the room, it suddenly all made sense to me. All of our pictures were no longer in sight. The few items of clothing I had left in the closet were no longer hanging. I got up and ran to the bathroom. As I figured, my toothbrush was gone, too. Nadine was not his 'ex' girlfriend! She was on her way to see her boyfriend! Jason started getting impatient. He grabbed the few things I brought with me and said he did not have time for my antics. I had never felt so low in my life. To him this was just another argument that would blow over as so many others had. He sped back to campus so fast that his car was rattling. He dropped me off without a word.

We hadn't spoken in over three weeks. I refused to answer his calls. He was calling to apologize and tell me how much he loved me but I was not about to let him off the hook that easily.

He was going to have to pay for what he did.

One of the guys in my engineering class, Omar, who was actu-ally pretty good looking, asked me out on a date. It was perfect. I would accept his invitation as a way of getting back at Jason. I just knew he would hear the news and realize what he had in me. But something happened. When I went on the date, I had the time of my life. It was nice. I hadn't laughed so hard in years. We had so much in common and by the end of the date, I knew I wanted to do it again. This was not part of my plan. It was only supposed to make Jason realize the error of his ways so that we would get back together. You see, I could not let Jason go. I could not desert him. When I got angry or disappointed in him I would think about all of the horror stories he shared with me about the cruel things his father had done to him when he was growing up. I just knew that his detached way of be-ing was not his fault and that eventually he would change. But something in me, a feeling more powerful than these thoughts, told me to go on another date with this new guy.

After about a week of spending every free moment with Omar, I was feeling great. I didn't know that a fun, caring and respect-ful relationship was possible. During the time that I shared with him, Jason didn't cross my mind. This was the most free I had ever felt.

Late one evening as Omar and I were hanging out in my dorm room, we heard a loud banging on the suite door. There were three rooms in my suite. The banging was so loud everyone came out of their rooms immediately. One of them looked out the peephole and told me it was Jason. He started demanding I come out as he was banging ferociously. He was yelling out at the top of his lungs that he knew I had someone in there and found every which way to call me a slut. I was mortified. As far as Omar knew, Jason was out of the picture. I did not know how to handle the situation. All I knew was that I could not feel any lower than I did in that moment. Omar asked me what this was all about and suggested we call the police. I said no, I did not want to cause that kind of trouble for Jason. After about 15 minutes, Jason stopped yelling and it appeared that he had left the area.

Omar and I spent the next couple of hours talking about my relationship with Jason and what led to this wild situation. He was really understanding about it. However, he made it clear that he did not agree with my decision about not calling the police. It was obvious to him that Jason was not acting rationally and had abusive tendencies. He really felt that I was in danger and that the police were the best way to protect me. As he was talking to me, he realized he was scaring me so he just held me in his arms until I fell asleep. I felt so safe.

At about 3AM that same night, we woke up to a tapping sound at the window. It was getting progressively louder when suddenly a rock crashed through the window. I knew right away that it was Jason. Omar was scared at this point. He knew he was in the middle of something that was out of his control. He waited until the morning and left with a meager hug and goodbye.

The next day Omar explained to me that he was in over his head and since our relationship was fairly new, he wanted out before it got too involved. He told me that he did not want to see me any longer.

I felt like the walls were closing in on me. I didn't have Jason or Omar in my life and it didn't feel good. Having a man in my life was very important to me. I loved the attention, feeling important and being accepted.

The phone rang and I picked it up on the fourth ring. It was Jason. My prayers had been answered! One minute he was begging me to come back to him and in the next he was expressing his anger. He kept asking me about this guy I was dating. I could hear his voice cracking in more vulnerable moments and it made my heart weak.

After going back and forth between his passive and aggressive behaviors, he started crying. It was the most unexpected reaction from him. That did it. He asked me to come over and I did. When I got there he was no longer crying and he had actually gotten hostile. He was angry at me for 'making' him cry. He grabbed me by the arm and took me into his bedroom. Before I could even lift a finger, he moved a dresser in front of the door to block me in. I had no clue what to expect because up until this point he had never been abusive with me. I mentally prepared myself for whatever was to come. He started asking me who the man was that I was seeing and I refused to answer him. I was not about to put Omar through any more drama. Jason was getting angrier by the minute. We were yelling back and forth when suddenly his name slipped out of my mouth. I had said "Omar" without even realizing it. Jason knew a little about the mystery man up to this point, so the first name was all he needed to find his phone number online. He went to reach for the phone and I grabbed his hand. Jason threw me on the bed and pinned me down at the legs and shoulders. At that point I started screaming frantically. The piercing sound was startling. He pulled his hand back in a motion to hit me and came down on my face so hard that my skull shook. I was stunned. It took me a few minutes for my ears to stop ringing and to focus my eyes. I could not believe he hit me. There was no controlling my screaming at this point. All he could do to calm me down was move the dresser and let me leave.

I was fuming. Looking like a woman that was slightly off-balance, I went over to his car and just stared at it as I tried to get my breathing under control. After contemplating for almost an hour whether to break his windows, slash his tires, or key it, I called the police to file a report.

The police met me at my dorm room. They spent the bulk of their time explaining to me the benefits of pressing charges against Jason because they knew that most women choose not to press charges in domestic violence situations such as this one. When the time came, I did not press charges.

Soon after that, I got back together with him and stayed for seven more months until I finally had it with the way he treated me.

TIME

So how many times did you say to yourself, what was she thinking? Get out of the relationship, run as far as you can and never turn back!? How about the very first choice I made to enter into the relationship even though he hadn't ended his existing relationship? Where was my self-love when I settled for half of a partner? Or how about when he could care less that I was hysterically crying? And how could I sleep with him despite the fact that he didn't even care about what happened to me?

As I look back at my life, sometimes I get bewildered by how low my self-esteem was. I didn't even realize that I had been abused way before he actually hit me. As if emotional neglect, manipulation and cruelty does not have the same ugly impact that physical violence does.

I simply did not think very highly of myself. I thought, "Hey, that man loves me and that is enough." But in any relationship where you do not have your dignity, respect and most importantly you are not able to be yourself, the love is only an illusion. It's an illusion that serves a distinct purpose. The purpose of avoiding yourself! I wanted to be in a relationship because then I would not have to deal with myself! By myself, I would actually have to spend time with myself. I would have to identify with myself. I would have to work on myself. I would have to take the time to get to know myself and I would have to show up in the world by myself. That simply did not sound appealing to me. I was not comfortable with being alone and unattached to someone else. The question then becomes, was the choice to avoid myself in my best interest? In other words, was it really serving me?

LO V E

*I*t is inevitable that life will throw us some curveballs. We cannot control everything around us even though most of us prefer to think we can. As tough as it may be, I believe it will serve you to let that notion go. But in the event that it is too unbearable to accept, I will tell you that there is something that you do have full control over. You have full control over the choices you make in the midst of all the happenings we call life. At any given time, you have the ability to make choices that serve you rather than work against you despite the circumstances. What then becomes difficult is deciphering what actually serves you! This is because choices are not always what they appear to be. There are choices that serve your highest good and there are choices that serve an immediate need. And to complicate things further, there is a distinction between a need and a desire, which many women gloss over, however, it is extremely important to know the difference when looking to get off your personal roller coaster.

You see, everything you *need* to live a loving, joyful and purposeful life is right there within you! The things you *desire* are meant to add to your life in an affirmative way.

During my ten year stint in a 9 to 5 career in Corporate America, I cannot tell you how many times I heard people say "I really *need* a cup of coffee." As if caffeine was the answer to making it through the day. What a farce. I guarantee there is no science book that says the human body relies on caffeine to function. But while I personally do not do caffeine, I can understand someone saying "I really *want* a cup of coffee" for whatever reason. Unfortunately, there are so many people addicted to caffeine not realizing that it is creating a long-term dependency rather than serving them, as it may appear in the short term. And it is because they are choosing it.

The choices you make are a clear reflection of how you feel about yourself. Our lives are composed of a string of *choice points* and, amazingly, if we were to examine them all we would see how we ended up where we are today. A choice point is simply a time in your life when you are faced with unlimited possibilities and you choose one. I say unlimited possibilities because with each unique situation there is an unlimited amount of ways to approach it, which includes all the ways that you *are* aware of and all those you are *not* aware of. We cannot quantify those possibilities that we are unaware of but we can explore them if we are open to stepping outside of our comfort zone. As uncomfortable as it sounds to step outside the realm of 'what you know' it is required when you want a new result. When you want something that has not yet occurred in your life.

I remember when I was scared to go to a restaurant by myself because I thought people would think I was a loser as if I had no friends or I couldn't find a man to take me out. I remember carefully planning to be on my cell phone or having a lot of paperwork to do so I could look important. But what I was really feeling was that I was unlovable by myself so I chose to be in relationships like the one I had with Jason. In fact, for seven years I continually entered into dysfunctional, damaging relationships. And because I did not choose to love myself, I was unaware that I had the strength, self-respect and confidence I needed to break this abusive cycle. And as uncomfortable as it was to stop getting into these relationships which acted as my decoy, when I finally did, it produced a whole new way of life for me. A life filled with positive, affirming and uplifting relationships. Up until then, I simply did not realize it was a matter of choice.

Here is a tip: *Making choices in your life that are harming you rather than helping you, is a clear sign that you do not love yourself fully. You run the risk of harboring deep-seated voids nurtured by years of conditioning from a culmination of negative experiences.* The most significant step in the journey to self-love is gaining the awareness that you are living without it. It is only then that you can choose do something about it.

Soon after a friend of mine participated in one of my work-shops, she shared a story with me. She remembered when I posed the question to the participants "Have you ever gone to eat at a restaurant by yourself and felt uncomfortable?"

She told me that she went to dinner with her sister at a trendy restaurant in Miami, Florida and there was a very attractive woman eating alone. At a table nearby, there were a mother and daughter enjoying their dinner. When it was time for the mother and daughter to leave, my friend saw them approach the woman who had been eating alone. The mother began to thank the woman for inspiring her because she never had the courage to eat at a restaurant alone. The mother continued to tell the woman how strong she thought she was and that she was glad her daughter had the opportunity to witness a woman with the courage and dignity to go out by herself.

I found her story fascinating for several reasons. I realized that women in particular have the tendency to notice a woman eating alone because subconsciously they do not find it socially acceptable. It is not "normal" to them and there must be some dire circumstances for them to do such a thing. The other realization I came to was that women find that it takes exceptional character to eat alone at a trendy restaurant where she will be noticed. As if a woman who does so has some sort of super powers and is unaffected by social criticism.

I loved the part of my friend's story when she told me that the mother went to acknowledge the woman for her strength and that she wants her daughter to be just as strong. Her heart was in the right place on both accords. But when she said that she would never have the courage to do it herself, she sold herself short. What she didn't realize is that she has the same possibilities for herself. We all have those qualities. We all have the ability to go to a restaurant simply because we want to and we all have the ability to feel great doing so. *It simply requires you to choose it. Once you have made the choice, the qualities you need to do it will show up. Remember everything you need is right there within you, it is simply a matter of accessing it when you are presented with the opportunity.*

Chapter 2

Is That Who I Say I Am?

> *"Trying hard to reach out*
> *But when I tried to speak out*
> *Felt like no one could hear me*
> *Wanted to belong here*
> *But something felt so wrong here*
> *So I pray I could breakaway"*
>
> - Breakaway, A song by Kelly Clarkson

 M E A N

I was home wondering where my boyfriend was, what he was doing and who he was with. On top of that, I was fuming that he would leave me home alone and go out without me. He finally reached my apartment around 10:30 p.m. looking very sexy. He was what one would consider a "pretty boy." Those men that take great care to ensure they always step out of the house looking good. He was excited about his evening and was raving about how much fun he had. To me it just sounded like boasting and like he was trying to make me mad. My stomach started to turn with all the thoughts going through my head. I felt like he was lying to me. I felt that this was really about him losing interest in me and that he was really out with another woman. I became concerned that he was going to break up with me.

It was exhausting holding all this in and I suddenly exploded. I blasted him with my thoughts and accusations. He just stood there with his mouth wide open wondering where this was all coming from. He thought to himself that I seemed fine when we agreed he would hang out with his boys that night. He interrupted my rampage and explained to me that he had no intention of letting me ruin his evening. He managed to give me a hug and headed home.

Soon after he left I called him to ask him to come back but he didn't answer. That bothered me even more. We had similar arguments in the past. He was aware of some of my insecurities that stemmed from past experiences and knowing all this kept him patient and understanding. I just knew he would give me a call the next day.

However, he did not call or even respond to my calls and I was not handling it well. I immediately worried that I had gone too far. He had it with my jealous rages and suspicious nature. I even started to realize how that could tick him off. I was starting to feel really bad about exploding the way I had. Not because of what I said and how I said it but because I thought this time he hit his limit. He was done with our relationship. I did not eat, sleep or talk to anyone. I even stayed home from work.

Two days later he called me first thing in the morning and acted as if we had never argued. He was super sweet and very loving.

I asked why he did not call me back and he reminded me that he was away on a business trip. I couldn't believe I forgot about that. I had worried myself sick for no reason. He asked me out to dinner that night and I quickly accepted. I was so relieved and immediately felt better.

Over the next couple months, things were going smoothly between us even though he was traveling a lot more on weekends and spending a lot more time hanging out with his boys. I decided I would keep my thoughts to myself about all the time apart to avoid any confrontation. I certainly did not want to push him away again. This was a big deal to me because I was pretty hot-tempered. I liked to duke it out rather than sweep things under the rug.

We had plans to spend a quiet evening at my place. I was excited to spend the quality time together. I even made his favorite meal and got two movies I knew he would love. When he arrived, I greeted him at the door, gave him a kiss and the first thing he said was, "We need to talk." He took my hand and guided me to the couch. I took a deep breath and braced myself for what was to come. I did not expect it to be anything good. For some reason I always expected the worst.

He held my hand as he proceeded to tell me that he wanted to break up with me. He did not see a future with me and felt that I needed time to heal from some of my experiences with men in the past. He felt he was getting some of the backlash and it was causing too much jealousy, distrust and arguing. This was not the type of relationship he was interested in. He felt it was time for him to play the field for a while. He wanted some freedom before he settled down with someone more suited for him.

My heart sunk to my foot. This was totally unexpected and I immediately felt terrible. I felt rejected, pathetic and stupid. I could not believe how blindsided I felt. I thought our relationship was going so well.

I asked him if he was sure about his decision and he said, "Yes." He had thought long and hard about it and realized he was not being fair to me. He loved me but he knew I was not "the one" so he did not want to be selfish by staying in the relationship. While I thought it was quite honorable of him to do so, since many men I knew would stay in the relationship while they did the searching and sowing, I was still devastated.

The next few weeks were rough. I felt so bad about myself and was starting to believe that I would never find a partner who truly loved me. I felt ugly, overweight, used, unfit, needy and hardened. Basically, I felt like damaged goods and did not want to do anything but drown in my sorrows. Rather than sharing these painful feelings with anyone, I decided to show up strong. So whenever I spoke to any of my friends I would proudly let them know that "he just lost the best thing he ever had!" and that he would eventually come running back to me.

About a month after our breakup I heard through the grapevine that he was seriously dating a young woman from out of town and it totally made sense to me then. He met her while we were still dating. His "playing the field" story was just that, a story. Instead of getting angry, I could not stop thinking about how lucky his new woman was to have him. I just knew she must have been prettier, thinner, more tactful, more independent and less tainted than me. It was apparent that my ex-boyfriend did not lose the best thing he ever had. I was sure he found someone better.

I look back on this relationship and still get confused. I was all over the place! I did not know whether I was coming or going. Was I a jealous person or simply insecure? Was I confident or just knew how to hide my feelings well? Was I aggressive or submissive? Was I an argumentative person or just someone who had not yet healed from her past? Did I really love this man or did I feel I needed him? Did I know how to communicate my feelings or did I just know how to react? I simply did not know the answers to these questions. I had no idea who I was. I was completely lost in all the unhealed pain that had compiled up to that point.

*O*n any given day, a woman can give a laundry list of things that she would like to change about herself, her life or her relationships. We even engage in lighthearted conversation about our lists. We sit with our girlfriends and gab about how we wish our butt was smaller, our boobs were bigger, our stomachs were flatter, we didn't have cellulite, we had more money or that we were more successful. It is perfectly fine to want to improve these aspects of ourselves but what we must be cognizant of is when these 'wishes' are expressing a feeling of inadequacy or a feeling of 'not being enough.' You see sometimes we are simply making conversation and don't realize that these desires, to change ourselves, are marinating within us making us really believe that we are not enough. "Not enough" to be loved just as we are! That is when our infamous 'self-esteem' is being affected.

The concept of self-esteem often gets a bad wrap. I have witnessed many people say that self-help books and personal development retreats, trainings, seminars or workshops are only for people with low self-esteem. When I first got into this line of work, I really searched for an answer to why people feel this way when in truth it is possible for anyone to benefit from self-help or personal development products and services. Simply put, they are tools that can assist us with discovering new things about ourselves. I quickly learned that people are afraid. People avoid looking within because they fear they may not like what they see. Unfortunately, if we are not open to exploring ourselves, no matter what the method, then we stay right where we are: making the same choices over and over, only the situation changes.

In all fairness, I believe the conversation of self-esteem is also off-putting because people tend to identify it in extreme states. Some people think having high self-esteem means you are conceited, egotistical or over confident. On the other end of the spectrum, some believe having low self-esteem is associated with being depressed, problematic, needy, pathetic or suicidal. None of which is necessarily true nor uplifting. The relationship between self-esteem and how we conduct ourselves is more comprehensive than that.

There are many interpretations and definitions for self-esteem. I gravitate to how self-esteem expert Nathaniel Branden interprets it. He says *"Self-esteem is the disposition to experience oneself as being competent to cope with the basic challenges of life and of being worthy of happiness. It is confidence in the efficacy of our mind, in our ability to think. By extension, it is confidence in our ability to learn, make appropriate choices and decisions, and respond effectively to change. It is also the experience that success, achievement, fulfillment — happiness — are right and natural for us. The survival-value of such confidence is obvious; so is the danger when it is missing."* Branden levels the playing field here. His premise is that we can all be confident in our abilities to approach life successfully and experience the joy that comes from it. The truth is that we are inherently worthy of this 'good life' at all times, however, we don't always feel like we are. I will go back to the newborn baby example. Remember we are as perfect today as the day we were born. This may be hard to imagine, especially if you are the survivor of a violent crime, but even abusers, rapists and murderers are intrinsically worthy. Unfortunately, hurt people, hurt other people. People who perform inhumane acts do not feel worthy of love, they are hurting whether consciously or unconsciously, and so they act out with these awful choices. This is where Branden's 'appropriate choices' comes into play. Most abusers have experienced some form of abuse themselves and rather than stop the cycle of abuse they choose to perpetuate it. People get to this breaking point for a myriad of reasons that we will explore further in the coming chapters.

What if we unceasingly felt worthy? No matter what someone says about you. No matter what has happened to you in the past. No matter how many mistakes you believe you have made. No matter what you see when you look in the mirror. No matter how hard it is to please your parents. No matter how much money you have. No matter what you do for a living. Whether you live in a ghetto or Beverly Hills, knowing you are worthy no matter what! How would it feel to know that none of it dictates your worthiness? It would probably remove those negative self-thoughts, beliefs and opinions from your mind. It is from this state of worthiness that it will feel natural to extend acts of love, kindness, generosity, peace and abundance to yourself and out into the world. If you find that you are not showing up in the world this way, then you want to evaluate whether you *feel worthy*, distinct from evaluating whether you *are worthy*.

I believe that self-esteem is rooted at the heart of a person. As a result, I define *self-esteem as the degree to which you love and express your authentic self.* When your heart is full of love your mind has the capacity to make constructive choices. Choices that are in alignment with your authentic self. The key is to know your authentic self, which is described as the core of who you are on the inside – your morals, your values, your spiritual-ity, your dignity and your integrity.

MORALS

Morals are the rules of action or conduct that you believe are good. Most textbook definitions of 'morals' entail the com-parison of right and wrong or good and evil. However, it is my belief that there is only one true nature in the world and that is good. In my experience, what creates wrong, bad and evil in the world are the experiences, interpretations, perceptions and misdirected anguish of human beings. For example, there is a general perception by humankind that there is not enough supply in the world, which leads to greed and withholding. As a result, people may react in various ways. They may focus on acquiring material things. They may equate status to success. They may do whatever it takes to make it to the top. They may beg, borrow or steal. They may go to war. They may kill. They may lie. All in an attempt to guard what they feel is rightfully theirs. However, what is actually theirs is the right to express their gifts, talents and treasures in a way that brings good to others but because of their misperception about supply they withhold, which leads to the breakdown of our society.

If our morals are grounded in all that is good, then that is what will show up in our consciousness, resulting in how we take action in the world. Some examples of morals are abundance, fidelity, abstinence, honesty, consistency, equality and reciprocity. Essentially they are any principles that you let guide your actions in life. I know of a woman whose life mission is to abolish the death sentence. She believes that murder is not the solution to criminal acts. Rather, she believes that all human beings should have the opportunity to learn from their mistakes during their lifetime. This is a strong stance and many people debate with her about it but she is clear on her moral position, so she is always up for the challenge.

VALUES

Values are those qualities that you find desirable or have an emotional investment in. Values may be positive such as love, peace, environmentalism, openness, freedom, education, health, authenticity or they can be negative such as hate, cruelty, greed, or blasphemy. However, as we discussed earlier, if you focus on all that is good then that is all that can show up through you. Values guide your ways of being and affect the choices you make.

For example, one of my core values is love. I do not choose to focus on hate. In fact, when my husband catches me saying, "I hate this computer, it keeps crashing on me!" he is quick to ask me, "What is all that hate about?" While I may get frustrated with him in the moment because he does not show any compassion by joining me in my 'throw this computer out the window campaign', I do realize the importance of not using the word. If I use the word hate then it exists to me and with the state of the world being what it is, we could use less recognition of hate. So no matter what situation comes my way, I try my best to address it from a loving place. This is not always easy and admittedly sometimes I have knee-jerk reactions that take over but I do my best. If necessary, I take time before addressing something so I can get grounded in love.

SPIRITUALITY

Spirituality is a holistic approach to the way you are connected with nature, the universe, God or however you identify a higher power in your life. Your spirituality is not your religion. Rather, religion is a subset of your spirituality. In other words, religion may be one of the ways you are connected to a higher power, but is not the only way. Spirituality encompasses your unique relationship with nature, the universe and a higher power, your awareness of this relationship, your practices and how you choose to express it.

Your relationship with a higher power is identified by the way you choose to relate to it. The human-higher power relationship varies anywhere from subordinate-authoritative to beneficiary-savior to student-example to embodiment.

The awareness of your relationship with a higher power will grow and unfold at whatever pace you do. That is why no two people have the same spiritual journey. While there are definitely relatable moments, it is important that you never compare your spiritual evolution to someone else's.

Your spiritual practices are those you choose to acknowledge and nourish this relationship in your life. Some common practices are prayer, meditation, attending church, identifying with a religion, participating in rituals and the recognition or use of symbols.

How you choose to express your spirituality is not how you spread the word about it. Actually quite the contrary, your spirituality is your own private sanctuary and is yours to share when you want to. However, spirituality shows up through your ways of being because it typically influences your morals and values.

My parents did a wonderful job of grounding me in the importance of being ethical, moral and having strong values without the introduction of religion or going to church on Sundays. This created the foundation for me to take my own "uninfluenced" spiritual journey and create my own relationship with God. I was able to define the role religion would take in my life. I also got to be awakened to my spiritual awareness in an organic way that made me confident that I am in alignment with my life's purpose. It was not always an easy journey, however. There were times, especially during my teenage years, when subconsciously I was seeking spiritual grounding. I was seeking answers or a knowing that there is some bigger reason for going through certain experiences—especially the unfavorable ones—and that there was some greater purpose for my being here. I distinctly remember asking "Why me?" at various points in my life and when all of the explanations offered by fellow humans did not seem to suffice, I felt confused and alone.

Acknowledging God in my life was a pivotal part of my journey. I remember taking a hard look at my life and realizing that with each event I went through, God was with me! It did not matter how seemingly bad the event was, there was a higher purpose for it. I went through it and came out stronger because there was a lesson God wanted me to learn. This realization helped me shift from a victim mentality to an empowered mentality. This new insight changed the types of questions I asked myself. I went from asking questions like "Why do all these bad things always happen to me?" to "What is the purpose of this event in my life?" Constantly doing the inner work to answer this question gave me information about who I am and my purpose here on Earth.

I share this overview of my spiritual journey with you to emphasize how important it is that you explore your own spirituality whether you grew up with a strong religious foundation or not. Again, spirituality is unique for every person.

DIGNITY

Dignity is your *innate* state of being worthy, respected, honored, or esteemed *and* it is your innate *right* to being respected. So if we are born worthy, respected, honored and esteemed then we can deduce that it is the happenings of life that can make us feel otherwise. But be sure to recognize that we only *feel* unworthy and that it is not the *truth* about us. Nonetheless, it takes a toll on the level of respect we have for ourselves. And as our self-respect takes a hit so does our ability to adhere to our *right* to be respected. This right is not generated from others or about other people's behavior, the right to be respected is about an individual respecting themselves enough to stand up for themselves, to monitor their self-treatment and self-talk, choose their relationships wisely and, in general, make choices that are in accordance with their state of worthiness, honor and esteem.

Have you ever been in a situation where you did not stand up for yourself? Perhaps someone said something negative about you and you let it slide? Perhaps you made yourself believe that it was not 'worth addressing' or 'you don't have time for such petty things.' Well each time you let someone say something other than the truth about you, you are defying your innate right to being respected.

This does not mean that in every situation you have to go address the person but the untruth about you must be cancelled out. In essence, you can do this by yourself just to make sure that your self-respect is unaffected. It can be as simple as someone telling me, "You are ugly" and all I would say to myself is "I am beautiful." I would not say this to retaliate but rather to affirm the truth about myself.

Growing up in Brooklyn, NY I always walked everywhere. In fact, I did not even get my drivers license until I was twenty-two years old. I can remember walking to the corner store for some random items needed at home and being propositioned by men in various ways. Some would be very friendly, some were aggressive and some were down right rude. Those that were friendly I would simply say something friendly back and be on my way but I would walk right by those that were aggressive or rude. There were lots of times when that would make them angry and I remember one particular time when one of them said to me "That's okay you're an ugly bitch anyway" and threw a cup of ice at me. I recognized that it would have been dangerous to say anything back so I picked up my pace and proceeded to the store. Later that day, I wondered what I did to deserve such treatment. Was I really ugly? Was I a mean person because I didn't respond to him? While I did nothing to deserve the rude treatment, where I did go "wrong" was in the conversation that went on in my own head. By questioning myself and giving their comments validity, I was compromising my own self-respect. Now I look back—knowing what I do now—and wish that I had told myself that I did nothing to deserve it and countered their commentary by telling myself that I was a beautiful young woman. Women lose their dignity on a daily basis when we believe other people's negativity and take it on as our own. The good news is that it is never too late to reverse any of these negative thoughts, beliefs or opinions.

INTEGRITY

Integrity is adherence to your morals, values, spirituality and dignity. In a thesaurus you will find synonyms like honesty or probity but I like to keep it simple and say its "Keeping your word!" If you commit to something then for gosh sakes, do it! People are not always aware of the significance in keeping their word especially in seemingly inconsequential situations. For example, if I tell someone I will meet him or her at the coffee shop at 2:00 pm and then show up at 2:15pm, by being late, I did not meet my commitment. Every time that a person does not keep their word they misrepresent themselves to the universe. They send a mixed signal to the world about who they are. Do you think this is an exaggeration? Are you saying to yourself, what does the world have to do with my being late to a coffee date? When I share this example in workshops or in coaching, most people do feel it is an exaggeration but I assure them there is truth to it. By being late, you are "telling" the person you met up with that they are not worth your commitment and that their time does not matter to you. Is that how you want to show up in the world? Is that the message you mean to send?

Isn't the example a bit more consequential now than when you first read it?

Now let me clear up a couple of things. If you are late to a date, I am by no means telling you to guilt and shame yourself. You can simply apologize and let them know that they matter to you. You can also call the person you are meeting to let them know that you are aware of the time and give them a progress report. However, there are commitments that when broken are much harder to recover from. For example, adultery, as your spouse could find you unworthy of trust. Or, missing a milestone event in your child's life, as you can be viewed as hurtful and uncaring. Defaulting on a loan, as you may be considered irresponsible. When making commitments, take the time to make sure you can keep your word and show up as the person you say you are.

These core aspects of your authentic self show up in your ways of being – the behaviors or attributes that you take on in your life on a daily basis. *It is when we stray from our authentic self that our self-esteem is susceptible to external influences.*

Chapter 3

If You Don't Know it's Broken...How Can You Fix It?

"There's no hiding place
When someone has hurt you
It's written on your face, and it reads
'Broken spirit, lost and confused'
'Empty, scared, used and abused, a fool'
Oh, ain't it funny that the way you feel
Shows on your face"

- My Sunshine Has Come, A song by Angie Stone

 M E A N

One year while I was in high school, I invited a friend to my house to celebrate Thanksgiving Day with my family. She had been on her own since she was four-teen years old so I really wanted her to feel loved by my family. Towards the end of the evening, I decided to walk her home, which was only a few blocks from my house, just across the street from my high school. I dropped her off, gave her a big hug and headed home. The air was brisk and heavy as I walked a familiar path that I had so many times before. I looked back for a moment and saw a man with a sweatshirt with a hood that was cocked slightly over his face. He was small in stature yet he appeared to be built. I couldn't see his face but I thought nothing of it and I proceeded on my way. He was about ten feet behind me when I saw him and before my face was even facing forward, suddenly his arm came swinging around my neck and he began to strangle me. Before I knew it, my forehead was against the ground and it was compressed so hard to the sidewalk that I could actually feel a bruise forming. I was thinking to myself that this was something that only happens in the movies. Was he about to strangle me until I took my last breath? Was he going to mug me or worse was he going to rape me? All this while my parents were less than a block away sipping coffee and eating pastries, none the wiser that their daughter was in such danger. Horrifying thoughts were running through my head a mile a minute. I saw a glimpse of a car slowing down right where we were and I guess he got scared that he would be seen and ran off. I blanked out. I was lying, bloody on the ground around the corner from a safe haven of family. Finally, some neighbors spotted me on the ground and helped me up. I was screaming for help at the top of my lungs. They persistently asked me where I lived. Although I was disoriented and hysterical, we managed to find my house.

I ran inside and when my parents saw me they had a look of horror on their faces. Here I was, their beloved daughter, with black and blue choke marks along my neck, broken blood vessels in and around my eyes, a large contusion along my forehead and blood running from my nose. My father and uncles grabbed bats and ran outside looking for the man who did this to me. My mom called the cops. When I described the perpetrator to them, they told my parents that this man had been named the

'East Flatbush Rapist' and had attacked seven women so far. I stayed home from school for about two weeks afraid to even leave my house. All my feelings of being young and invincible were erased from my programming. Three weeks after the traumatic event, the rapist had been arrested as he was attacking his ninth victim.

T I M E

*T*his was a painful event in my life that I never truly understood the impact of until much later in life. In fact, after being attacked by the East Flatbush Rapist, more traumatic events manifested in my life and I kept experiencing them without taking the time to process and heal: I did not reflect on each experience to seek out the lessons. I did not recognize whether I was being myself or pretending to be someone that other people wanted me to be. I did not decipher what I made up in my head about the experience versus what actually happened. I did not make the connection that my choices, at times, would lead to some of the hurtful events. And when that was the case, I did not accept responsibility for my role in it. I did not forgive myself and others for what happened. Instead the pattern just continued and my self-esteem continued to take a nose dive with each experience. Because I did not love myself nor feel worthy of love, I managed to get myself into one poor relationship after another thinking that love from someone other than myself would fix all that.

From the outside looking in, I had everything else in my life going on! I attained a Bachelor of Engineering, a Master of Science in Engineering and got into an esteemed Engineering program at a Fortune 500 company that paid quite well. I continued on to work in several lucrative positions all the while getting myself into self-destructive relationships that no one really knew the true nature of because everything else in my life was going so well. I was even mentoring young girls, volunteering on weekends to help inner city youth prepare for their SATs, tutoring at community colleges and much more. I made it virtually impossible for anyone to know the internal turmoil I was going through unless I shared it with them.

I grew up in a loving, close-knit family and even they did not know the full extent of what I was going through. My parents bestowed upon my sister and I, all of the love they had in them. They provided a solid foundation for us to know what love is and what it feels like. It is my opinion that if parents teach their children to love themselves and that they are loved, then they have done a great job! As evident by what I have been through, this does not necessarily protect us from danger, hurt or misfortune, but it does serve as a point of reference for us to know the truth about ourselves as we go through life. You see, *it is not the events or circumstances in life that hold any truth about us, but rather it is our capacity to love and be loved that is real, and it starts with loving ourselves!*

Unfortunately, not everyone has parents that know how to demonstrate love. This can definitely be a setback but the good news is that there is a constant flow of love moving through the universe. People are constantly exchanging love. They are either giving it, receiving it or asking for it. You can get to know love by tapping into that flow anytime, any place and with anyone. If you choose to do so, love will show up.

L O V E

*H*ow does a woman get to a point where she does not love herself? What compels a woman to stay in an abusive relationship? Or what makes an anorexic woman continue to starve herself? Or a bulimic woman to continuously purge her body of necessary nutrients? Or drug addicts to continue to inject poison into their body? *The answer is it starts with something external that we end up internalizing and then we get the false sense that this feeling is real. In other words, all of the people, experiences and things that we engage in our lives have the ability to sway our opinions, beliefs and feelings about ourselves.*

PEOPLE

People play a significant role in our self-esteem. Relationships are a constant in life. Every relationship is unique in its own right and they are virtually impossible to avoid. They vary from being innately strong and deep, to the consequence of day-to-day interactions in the world. Did you know you are in a relationship with your mail carrier? It may seem like an inconsequential relationship but if you think about it, you depend on him or her to receive information from other people that are looking to connect with you. Don't get me wrong, this relationship is not as significant as the one you have with your intimate partner but nonetheless it is a relationship. Understanding all of the relationships in your life can really help you appreciate the countless opportunities we have to give and receive love. You would be surprised what a simple "Thank you" can do for a mail carrier or anyone who provides service to us, that we sometimes take for granted. That expression of gratitude is an act of love. You can put a smile on someone's face that easily. It is actually that simple to express love to anyone but life happens and we let things like emotions, expectations and judgments get in our way.

One of the most influential relationships of all is the one we have with our parents. No matter what the condition of the relationship is between a parent and their child, it is extremely strong. This is why children, who have been abused or abandoned by their parents, still crave love from them. This is also why many adopted children desire to meet their biological parents no matter how much time has passed or how amazing their adoptive parents are. The relationship with our parents can be a good or bad influence. If your parents are extremely affirming and loving then it is helpful. But if your parents are aloof, negative or abusive then it can be a blow to your self-esteem. I cannot tell you how many women I have come into contact with, that to this day, in their adulthood, have not forgotten, forgiven or released harmful things their parents have said about them or done to them. By no means do I think that it is easy, but I do believe it is necessary that we work through any deep-seated issues we have with our parents. Doing so is the key to releasing the belief that you are not worthy of respect and dignity from anyone who comes into your life, including your parents.

In the last episode of my favorite television show of all time, *Sex and the City*, the main character says, "But the most exciting, challenging and significant relationship of all is the one you have with yourself." If you know anything about the show, you know that she discovers this after she goes through a barrage of unsuccessful relationships. It is innate to want companionship and to find our "soul mate," but I find it fascinating that we tend to seek it out at any cost! I know it feels absolutely great to be in love, but you have to know that it is much more complex than this. Outside of the desire to share pure and equitable love with someone, the desire to have someone in your life stems, anywhere, from searching for social acceptance to the avoidance of dealing with one's own issues. This is why I love the character Carrie because over the course of the *Sex and the City* series she takes you through all the machinations women go through to find "The One". The problem is that as we go through this journey, we meet all types of people that may or may not be for us. Who may or may not, at a minimum, care about our well-being. And so we can get ourselves into situations where we are vulnerable to what a person thinks about us, says about us or does to us. And since they are our 'significant other' that we want so badly to be 'The One', we tend to make it all true, the good, the bad and the ugly. As you read on, you will learn the underlying reasons why this happens.

But before we move on, let me just say that Carrie nailed it when she said the most significant relationship we have is the one we have with ourselves. The relationship with self often goes unnoticed because we take it for granted and there are simply too many distractions to take our focus off of it. But the love and bonding we have with ourselves is the most impacting relationship of them all. It is the glue that keeps all other relationships together. If the relationship with yourself is lacking then all other relationships will suffer.

FEEDBACK

It would be remiss of me not to discuss the concept of feedback at this point because this is a situation where what people have to say about you can serve you. Feedback is when people or groups of people provide insight about a process or activity that can be forwarding whether it seems positive or negative. The keyword is *forwarding*. For example, let's say you gave an important presentation at work. Afterwards your peer tells you that you did a great job. He also mentions that you move your hands quite a bit while you present which can be distracting for the audience. How would you feel? Would you be offended, angry, hurt or sad? Or would you think of it as constructive information that could help you? In this situation, your peer provided you with feedback and what you do with it is totally up to you. The problem is that many people do not handle well, what appears to be negative feedback. They get emotional about it rather than thinking clearly about whether there is some truth to it and whether they can benefit from it.

There are two main reasons for this. One is that the ego can get in the way. The ego is the entity of ourselves that protects how we are presented in the world primarily on a superficial level. The ego wants to obliterate anything that does not make us look good and normally jumps to a knee-jerk reaction rather than a well thought out response.

The other reason people do not handle feedback well is if they have low self-esteem as I define it – they do not love themselves fully. If this is the case, then they consciously, or unconsciously, interpret the feedback as negative. Rather than see if there is an opportunity to grow from what was said, they decide that it means something must be wrong with them or that they have done something poorly.

I want to make a clear distinction: Feedback is different from someone randomly giving an opinion of you that does not serve you. Feedback can serve you but it is up to you to view it that way and distinguish what, if anything, you can learn from it.

It may help to know that feedback is not the truth, it is simply information.

EXPERIENCES

Experiences also play a significant role in how we feel about ourselves. From the moment we arrive in the world we are impressionable and susceptible to what happens in our lives. Whether they are experiences that we choose to have or experiences that happen to us, we are constantly collecting data on how we feel about ourselves. And with each experience we "make up" what it means about ourselves. Unfortunately, when it is a negative experience we have the tendency to think the worst like "I deserved it" or "It's because I am ugly" or "It's because I am fat" or "It's because no one loves me" and these types of thoughts have the ability to spiral us into self-destructive actions.

In the work I do with teenagers, I have found that one out of every four young ladies I encounter has experienced some form of sexual abuse. It is a large-scale epidemic that is growing by the day. In addition to the damage done by the violence of this act, girls don't even have the opportunity to catch up with their sexuality before they are exposed to such a twisted idea of what it is. Most of the time these girls are too young to know how to process what occurred to them so they go through life feeling wounded, until they learn ways to heal. Research shows how influential a painful experience can be. Survivors of sexual assault are three times more likely to suffer from depression; six times more likely to suffer from post-traumatic stress disorder; thirteen times more likely to abuse alcohol; twenty-six times more likely to abuse drugs; four times more likely to contemplate suicide.[2]

I recall a young lady who participated in one of my camps for teenagers. She was obese and seemed to be proud of it. While I admired her confidence, I was concerned about her health. I believed she was hiding behind her weight and using food to cover up a deep rooted issue.

When the opportunity presented itself, I had a conversation with her. I opened by asking whether she believed she had healthy eating habits and whether she believes she takes care of her body. She quickly responded by telling me that she doesn't care how she looks and that she was going to eat whatever she wants to. I asked her why she did not care about her appearance or her general health. She proceeded to tell me that she did not want to bring any attention and more importantly did not want to attract anyone to her. I kept asking her why until we drilled down to the fundamental reason she was obese. Her uncle raped her when she was nine years old and continued to do so for years. As she released this deep dark secret, I held her in my arms and we cried. She had been using the extra weight as a shield, a protector, to avoid any relationships with men. She did not want to be attractive. Her view of relationship, sex and attraction was so distorted, rightfully so, due to her experience.

THINGS

When I was a teenager, I experimented with bulimia. Bulimia is an eating disorder that involves eating, or binging, and then purging the food by self-induced vomiting, extreme exercise, laxatives or fasting.[3] Among my friends in high school, it was the "cool" way to stay thin. After witnessing the binge and purging process several times, I tried it myself. One day after eating a sizable meal, I went to the bathroom and made myself vomit.

The experience was gross but I actually felt satisfied afterwards. According to what I thought was attractive, the skinnier I was, the better. Those days I was starting to get curves in places that I never imagined and I thought they made me look chunky. I certainly hadn't seen those kinds of curves on the covers of magazines or in any of my favorite music videos. It wasn't until a friend of mine got very sick from bulimia that I realized the severity of it and I stopped. But for years thereafter I contemplated purging whenever I felt inadequate.

Mainstream media is the perfect example of something that has the power to make us feel bad about ourselves. It is an external factor that manages to make women uncomfortable in their own skin because every woman on the cover of a magazine, in a commercial, acting in movies, singing in videos, is a size two or smaller. In the media, women are impeccably made up with makeup, perfectly styled hair and expensive clothing that is nine times out of ten tailored just for them. Not to mention, air brushing is used to cover their perceived flaws. These attractively made-up images have become the standard of "beauty" in our society and because most of us do not look like that, we emotionally and many times physically beat ourselves up over it. Along with the media, societal pressures add to the mass generalizations, misperceptions and the "I'm not enough" thinking. For example, there is a notion that a woman must have an intimate partner in order to be socially acceptable. This causes some of us to do whatever it takes to conform to what we believe is needed to be attractive and the longer it takes to find that person, the harder and more judgmental we get about our looks. Our society is so preoccupied with appearance that plastic surgeons are now offering payment plans! I remember a past hairdresser of mine telling me that she and her best friend were about to get breast augmentations for only $79 per month.

So what are women left to conclude if we don't look like we stepped out of a magazine? We "make up" that it means we are not beautiful. And as long as we feel that way, we go through life struggling to meet these fabricated standards of beauty that are leading to epidemics of eating disorders, low self-esteem, dependency and depression.

Exploitation of women has hit an all-time high. Dr. Mary Pipher, author of *Reviving Ophelia: Saving the Selves of Adolescent Girls*, says "the gap between girls' true selves and cultural prescriptions for what is properly female creates enormous problems."[4] In this era, adolescent girls are so highly influenced by the use of sex in the entertainment industry that it has become cool to be sexual at an early age. Every time I turn around, I see a teenage actress or singer, half clothed on the covers of magazines, on TV shows or in videos. I hear about teenage girls getting breast augmentations before their natural size has even matured. The influence is extremely strong. "By age 15, more than a third of American girls say they are sexually active, according to a Centers for Disease Control and Prevention survey. About 26% have had oral sex, 26% have had vaginal intercourse, and another 8% have had oral sex without intercourse. The proportion that is sexually active grows substantially every year thereafter."[5] The pressure to be sexually active seems insurmountable these days. A young lady does not even have the chance to develop the mental capacity it takes to enter into a healthy sexual relationship before she is thrown into it by social pressure. Fundamentally, at such a young age she is not yet aware of the meaning of true love and partnership nor the health responsibilities or consequences of entering into a sexual relationship. Without this awareness, it is difficult to make sound choices. While some young relationships thrive there are many that end devastatingly. She may end up being rejected by the person she had sex with. She may contract a sexually transmitted disease. She may get pregnant leading to the responsibility of being a teenage mother or having an abortion. There are many more possible scenarios but my point is that all of them lead to detrimental feelings like self-disdain, guilt or regret. And to make things worse, girls are avoiding these feelings by entering into more sexual behavior. They find comfort in the popularity among boys or the mistaken feeling of love or the self-deprecating nature of the behavior. These are just some of the ways the entertainment industry is impacting the self-esteem of young girls.

To summarize, the power of external influences can be difficult to overcome. If we do not know how to deal with them effectively, we will allow people, things and past experiences, especially painful ones, to mold how we lead our lives.

Oh How I love Thee, Let Me Count the Ways... to Fill a Gap

Chapter 4

"Everywhere I'm turning
Nothing seems complete
I stand up and I'm searching
For the better part of me
I hang my head from sorrow
Slave to humanity
I wear it on my shoulders
Gotta find the strength in me"

- Superwoman, A song by Alicia Keys

MEAN

John was so good to me. I did not believe that a man could treat me so wonderfully. This was like a storybook romance. In fact I was sure I had read about what he did for me on Valentine's Day in one of those Danielle Steele books. We had been together for just about a year and so he wanted this Valentine's Day to be very special. He took me to one of the finest restaurants in the area. We had a great view of the city, great food and great conversation. I was thinking to myself that this was by far the most money any guy had ever spent on me and I was blown away by the effort he put into planning the evening. When we got to his apartment, it was dark inside. As I walked into the hallway he says "hey sweetie, will you help me get some of these lights" and tossed me a lighter. I caught it just as coolly as he tossed it. When it started to get brighter in the room, I realized that there were candles all over and he was lighting them one by one. Blown away, I started to light some too. When I looked down at the floor, I realized I was stepping on rose petals! The room was so beautiful! When I made my way to the living room there was a huge basket set up with gifts, champagne and Blockbuster movies. He knew how much I loved movies and so he made it the most romantic Blockbuster night possible.

The next day while I was relishing in the wonder of the evening, the phone rang and I was faced with a big dose of reality. It was my boyfriend calling to let me know that his parents will be coming in to town next week to visit him. He told me that he was not ready for me to meet them and that he would not see me until they left. John's parents believed he should only get into relationships with women of his own ethnicity because it was tradition to marry within their culture. I knew this about him but I let it slide because this was the best I had ever been treated. I also felt that his love for me would transcend the cultural barrier and eventually he would bring me home to his mother.

As our relationship unfolded, our love continued to grow. We couldn't keep our affection a secret. We were known as the couple that everyone wanted to be like – young, successful and good looking. There was one thing that continued to bother me though. He still had not taken me to meet his parents and we were going on two years together. I knew he was crazy about me but at times I felt that perhaps he was using me. When he was courting me, I had been one of the girls that all the guys in our circle wanted to date. This led me to feel like a showpiece at times rather than his girlfriend. And the longer it took him to take me seriously, the more the feeling grew.

Eventually, I couldn't help but let my insecurities get the best of me. I officially believed that he had no intentions of taking the next step with me. Rather than talk to him about it and let him know that it was important to me, I stayed in the relationship and became less and less sure of myself. I started to get jealous of other women in his life. I got upset whenever he chose to hang out with his friends over me. And whenever the subject of his parents came up, we had an argument.

John did not understand why I was acting this way. It seemed to him that I wanted to argue just for the sake of arguing. He could not stand any type of conflict and it was starting to wear thin on him. Since he knew he would never marry me, he finally broke it off when he felt the lows were outweighing the highs of the relationship.

This hurt me terribly and I desperately wanted him to stay with me. In fact, for the next several weeks I kept calling him and begging him to get back together. I felt pathetic.

I did not eat for two weeks straight and besides the obvious health impact of that, I had been drinking and smoking cigarettes in its place. This was taking a toll on my body especially since I was working twelve hours a day, seven days a week. One night as I was resting in my apartment my heart started to race. It was a heart condition that I had since I was eleven but this time it seemed like it was back with a vengeance. No matter what I tried, I could not get it to slow down. I realized I had to go to the hospital. I had no close friends at the time because I had put them all on the back burner over the course of my relationship with John. And since all of my family lived out of state, the only person I could turn to was him. He took me to the emergency room where I was treated immediately. They told me if I had waited any longer I would have been in a lot worse shape. I thought to myself, if they'd only known the half of it.

chose to be with John because he treated me better than the men in my past relationships. He was a rock star compared to the rest of them. What I didn't realize was that I did not feel worthy of more. Like having the entire package of being treated well, meeting the parents and even marriage. I remember thinking 'he will never marry me.' And now I think, well why the heck did I stay with him when there was a limitation on how far he would go with me?

To many, it did not make sense that a woman who seemed to have it all together could not get her relationships right. I was pretty, healthy, excelled in my education, on the fast track in my career and I cared about the world. While my choices in men did not seem to match up to that exterior, they were actually a perfect reflection of what I felt I deserved. *They were a perfect reflection of my self-evaluated worthiness.* Don't get me wrong, all the great things in my life were also a reflection of me but the red flag that something was not quite right with Anita was my relationships. A red flag that was easy to dismiss because I had the comfort of a life that appeared to be working. To many I had it all. What people did not know was that I let my self-esteem get so low with each relationship that passed by, I was digging myself deeper and deeper into a hole. So when I finally did make the choice to find out what was underneath all of these poor decisions, I hit rock bottom before I worked my way out of that hole. It is often said that drug addicts must hit rock bottom before they will even attempt to get clean. Well that was exactly where I was but instead of drugs my addiction was unhealthy relationships with men. I remember the last boyfriend before my turning point. He put a gun to my face and told me that I would never find someone who loved me as much as he did.

On my path to recovery, I discovered a new concept that I call *gaps*. *Gaps are breaks in self-love that are caused by an unfavorable feeling or set of feelings we have about ourselves.* I learned that it is not people that are broken; it is self-love that can be broken. Gaps do not physically exist rather they exist in our consciousness. When a woman is operating with gaps, she does not love herself fully. At this time, she is not embracing the truth that she is perfect, whole and complete. And so she lives her life as if she is not enough. She lives her life as if she is not worthy of any good. Living this way leaves us yearning for whatever it is that can make us feel good. Unfortunately, it is not instinctive to know that all we need to do is love ourselves fully to actually feel worthy, so we turn outside of ourselves.

We choose external things, actions or relationships to fill gaps. We create *fillers*. The anomaly is that when operating with gaps the only choice that is going to produce healthy experiences, actions or relationships in your life is to fill them with your own love so we end up choosing fillers that do not serve us. *In other words, fillers that lead to unfavorable consequences that are physically or emotionally damaging or some combination of these.*

Fillers range from being obvious to being virtually undetectable. When a woman is addicted to drugs or alcohol, there is a red flag that screams "I do not love myself!" It is intuitive that anyone who would continually put harmful chemicals in her body does not love herself. Another example is a woman who stays in a physically abusive relationship. She can see the bumps and bruises yet she continues to stay with her abuser. When a woman suffering from anorexia becomes skin and bones, you can tell that she does not care enough about herself to give her body the nutrients it needs to thrive. A smoker knows that she is inhaling a toxin that is proven to kill yet she does it anyway. A compulsive gambler can blow away her life savings, her home or her car in one evening but nine times out of ten she will be right back at the casino the next night. How about cutters? Cutting your own body is a blatant indication of low self-esteem. And the ultimate demonstration of self-disdain is when one commits or attempts suicide. She no longer feels worthy to live.

Fillers become more difficult to detect when everything seems to be going well for a person. It's like the woman who has a successful career and is making a lot of money but walks around the office mean and miserable. She works more than she plays, she belittles people more than she uplifts them and she complains more than she solves problems. One does not immediately think that she is unhappy with herself because what they know is that she has status and power which many equate to fulfillment. Meanwhile, this woman is filling her gaps with her career. If she loved herself, and her life, that is just how she would show up. She would be loving, joyful and supportive around the office.

While I met many disgruntled people over the course of my corporate career, I particularly recall a young woman who used to sit at her desk and on any given day, I didn't know if it was okay to approach her. It was like grumpiness exuded from her, forming a cloud around her cubicle. She may as well have put a sign up saying "Enter at your own risk." If you asked her a question on one of these days, she would turn around and give you the look of death. I would dread going to her for anything simply because I couldn't stand to see someone so miserable. One day I decided I had enough of her attitude contaminating the office so I wrote her an email that simply said "Are you okay?" She wrote back that she has been trying to have a baby for close to a year and was starting to get worried that she cannot conceive. She even asked me how long it took me to get pregnant. So I wrote her back assuring her that everything will be okay and even gave her some coaching about how her attitude affects the office that she was grateful to receive. From that day forward, attitude or not, I always had a smile for her because I understood that she was hurting.

How about the woman that stays with her boyfriend for years upon years because she is too comfortable to start over? Meanwhile her relationship is unsatisfying, superficial and lacks sizzle but because it has longevity, it appears to be a healthy situation. Simply put, she is settling. Her boyfriend is actually the filler. She is holding herself small because she does not feel worthy of finding the love of her life, someone who will love her the way she truly desires. This is an all too common scenario.

There are two ways we operate with gaps: consciously and unconsciously. The difference between the two is that, simply put, in one way you are aware that you are making choices based on negative feelings and the other you are not. Unfortunately, the more common is when you are not aware.

When you are aware that you are making poor choices to make yourself feel better and can connect it with a negative feeling about yourself, then you are consciously filling gaps. One example that I typically use to demonstrate this conscious behavior happens when women go shopping for clothes. When women go into the fitting rooms to try on clothes and look in the mirror, it is as if the lighting in the fitting room is designed to pick up every flaw on our being! We immediately blame the lighting but, of course, find some truth in what we are seeing. I cannot tell you how many times I have immediately felt bad about myself and chose to run up my credit cards just to buy more clothing that could perfectly cover up the awful sight I just saw. I know this to be true for others because I have shared many laughs about this with friends who have experienced the same. Okay so we shared a giggle or two, but when you really think about it, we were carrying out harmful behavior, which in this case was racking up our credit card bills, to hide how imperfect we felt our bodies were – the negative feeling. So we made a conscious decision to spend money we did not have, knowing that we did not feel good about ourselves.

Here's another example. Have you ever had a person in your life that you call a friend but deep down you know they are not good for you? They don't support your dreams, they are a bad influence on you or they make insulting remarks about you. But on a day where you feel lonely you choose to hang out with them anyway. Feeling lonely usually translates to "I do not want to spend time by myself" and in this case you would rather spend time with someone who is no good for you.

When you consciously fill gaps, you are able to rationalize and analyze your behavior. And is it just me or do women love to analyze? We manage to convince ourselves and others that making a poor choice is really the thing to do. In fact, it is the right thing to do! We make up that burying the bad feeling about ourselves is best for us. *The truth is that it is never a good idea to ignore your feelings no matter how inconsequential it may seem because your feelings, left unaddressed from within, will shift your perspective of who you are. This is precisely how gaps are formed.*

After I was raped, I pushed the experience out of my consciousness so that I could go on as if it never happened. To this day, I don't really know how I did it. While I thought it was working for me, all the while it was taking residence in my subconscious making me feel unworthy and ultimately created a gap. The gap manifested in another abusive relationship.

Unconsciously filling gaps has more severe consequences than when you are aware of what you are doing because it is hard to fix something that you don't know exists. You can go on for years making a detrimental choice, or choices, not realizing that you are filling gaps. As a result, you don't even know to look for the signs that you are in a situation that is not serving your highest good. Consequently, you are not triggered to look within and discover why you are making such a choice.

I chose to stay with John even though he did not love me as I desired, or deserved, because subconsciously I wanted him in my life at any cost. I did not love myself fully and knowing he loved me, made me feel complete. Unfortunately, I paid the prices of experiencing hurt and humiliation, going into a self-destructive tailspin and ending up in the hospital with an out of control health challenge.

When operating with gaps, you will always pay prices.

I know a woman who stayed in her marriage with a very domineering man for so long that she let her childbearing years pass her by without having children. It had always been her dream to have children but it was not her husband's. She spent many years trying to change his mind but he never budged. Instead he found other ways to appease her. It must have worked because she continued to stay in her marriage and ignore her true desire. When the point came that she could no longer have children, she was devastated. She often tried to talk to her husband about her feelings but rather than listen and be supportive he made light of the situation. He spoke of all the freedom and disposable income they had as a result of not having children. She did not even have a compassionate shoulder to cry on as she cast her dream aside. She had a "marriage" but paid the ultimate price of never having her own children.

I know what I am about to say is nothing new but it must be said. *When we hang on to "Past Due" relationships, we close our doors to the possibility of healthier and grander relationships.* The hardest thing to say to a woman in the middle of a breakup especially from a marriage with many years invested is "You'll get over it and you'll find someone better matched for you." Because while it is true, it is not what women want to hear in that moment. It implies too much work. Imagine having to overcome all of the current pain; taking a deep look within; potentially spending some time alone; putting yourself out there again and then getting to know someone all over again! What I will simply say for now is, "Why not?"

Chapter 5

You Can Run But You Can't Hide

"Went through the same point
Of givin' up
I felt like I had enough
Went to the edge of the ledge
But I didn't jump"

- Good Woman Down, A song by Mary J. Blige

 M E A N

*H*e loved me so much but in my heart I knew he was not the one for me. There were so many indications that we were not equally matched but it was way more comfortable for me to stay in the relationship than to get out. It wasn't until I started feeling like I was using him that I chose to break up with him. I felt so ashamed of myself that I really believed I was a terrible person.

He was still in the process of making me feel like the scum of the earth for leaving him when I moved to a new state for a new job. I took this opportunity to start anew. I purposefully engaged in a lighthearted lifestyle because I wanted to be free of anything that felt heavy. So I spent my time doing things like dining out, shopping, bowling, networking, traveling and non-committal dating. It was working out fine until one day, unbeknownst to me, I opened the door wide open for turmoil to make its way right in.

A really nice guy named Tom had been expressing his interest in me for quite some time and up to this point I really had not paid much attention to him. Not just because he wasn't my type but it just so happened he was married.

On a day I was feeling particularly bad about myself after quite a heated call from my ex-boyfriend, I attained a hairline fracture in the wall I had built against all of Tom's acts of kindness. Tom asked me to go to lunch with him and this time I said yes. I felt like I needed some positive attention.

At lunch, Tom explained to me how he could not get me off his mind. He thought about me constantly and was not sure what to do about it. He also explained that his marriage was in pieces and they were on the verge of a separation. He said the main thing stopping him was that he had a child that he did not want to be apart from, not even for a moment. I thought that was honorable.

Months went by with Tom continuing to express his feelings for me and it was starting to break me down. It did not matter what I did to distract myself, I got to the point where I relied on his attention to feel good about myself. He was in tune with what I wanted to hear and the types of things I appreciated. I finally accepted one of his invitations to go to a party. He assured me I would be whisked to the front of the line and would have all my drinks paid for throughout the night. I could even bring a friend. We ended up having a blast. I was immediately impressed with how far he would go to make sure I had fun and to treat me like a lady.

The next day I could not help but feel bad about going on a date with another woman's husband and decided that no matter what, I was not going to spend anymore time with him. Then he called later that day and asked if I wanted to go to another party. The first one was so much fun that I decided to go. I just told myself that we would not cross the friendship line.

While I was conflicted about spending time with Tom, I was now addicted to the attention and the non-stop high-profile lifestyle. Before I knew it, we were taking surprise getaways where he also rolled out the red carpet.

I was officially caught up in a mess. He kept assuring me that he and his wife were sleeping in separate rooms and solely staying in the house together for the sake of their son but I was not satisfied with that. My anger and frustration became uncontrollable. I was mad at him and madder at myself. As a result, every other day I would go off on a tirade, yelling and screaming at him, blaming him for getting me into this mess and I would end up breaking up with him. It was as if we went to war every other day. However, he knew all the right buttons to push to get back in good standing with me. As a result, we were literally on one day and off the next, leading to an extremely tumultuous ride together.

Finally, I put my foot down and told him he needed to choose between me and his wife. He ended up moving in with a friend but spent a lot of time at home because he wanted to see his son. I didn't mind as long as he was not spending the night there.

One night while he was at my house, my phone rang. I picked it up to find that the person had hung up. It rang three more times with the same result. I looked at my caller ID and saw that it was coming from his house. My heart fell to my feet. I never meant for it to get to this point. I did not want to hurt his wife and definitely did not want to be in conflict with her. Later the phone rang and his wife said "Put my husband on the phone." I was so startled. How did she know he was here? I ran to the window to see her standing outside of my house. She was on her cell phone. This was absolutely insane. It was like a scene from a movie.

Tom went outside. I watched as he instructed his wife to get back in her car and leave. His wife said "only if you come with me." He looked up at the window, looked directly in my face and left.

I could not believe it. Had he been lying to me all this time? Were they still together? And if so, his wife had every right to come fetch her husband from my house. I was so angry I felt sick.

It was time for me to make a decision and stick with it. I decided that it would help get my mind off Tom, if I started to date again. I had been with Tom a year already and despite the shame, guilt and exhaustion I felt, I loved him and I was going to miss the good times we had. When I told him I was done, he did not take it well. He started to call me twenty times a day telling me how he could not live without me. He would get drunk and drive all over the city and call me at odd hours of the night. He said things to manipulate me like "If we were together, I wouldn't have to drink like this." It tore me up to think that I was the reason he was behaving like this, not to mention that I was scared for myself. He was circling my house several times a night. On top of that, his wife was making trips by my home too, thinking that he must be with me if he wasn't at home.

I had never felt so low. The situation was totally out of control but the one thing I did have control over was who I would date next. I met a really nice guy at one of my business meetings and decided he was it. The perfect distraction from the mess I had made of my life.

We went on several dates and had instant chemistry. Our favorite pass time became watching movies at his house. It was refreshing to be able to go to his house! A liberty as simple as that felt so good to me. This was great. Even though Tom was still stalking me, I had something good going here with this new guy.

Two weeks had passed when I got a call from Tom and he was angry as hell. I did not know what was going on so I tried to calm him down so that he would be coherent. It turned out that Tom had heard I was dating someone new and it was someone from his inner circle! He told me he was on his way over to my house. When he arrived, he was banging on the door wildly. I was so embarrassed of what the neighbors would think that I opened the door. He barged in and pulled out a gun. He pointed it directly in my face and told me that he should kill me right there on the spot. He was so angry he looked possessed. It was horrific. At this point, I was numb. I knew that it was wrong for me to have ever gotten involved with him in the first place, but I did not know I would die for it. Although, at this point the idea did not seem so bad. I had had it with my life. I was never going to find someone to love me and simply did not feel like living anymore. I had no idea what he was going to do to me. He proceeded to tell me how much he loved me and that no man could ever love me as much as he does. He finally calmed down and put his gun away. As I let all this soak in, I found myself hoping to God he really loved me that much.

Over the next few days he called me numerous times to tell me that he could not live without me. I had been working on a huge presentation for work and even though I knocked it out of the park, by the end of the week, I was ready to relieve some stress. When Tom called to ask me out, I took him up on his offer. Before I knew it I was back in the swing of things with him. Just like old times.

It was 1:00 am when I was awakened by Tom yelling outside of my front door. I asked him to keep it down so that my neighbors wouldn't hear him but he kept getting louder. I could tell he was drunk and I remembered what happened last time he was in a similar state but once again I was so embarrassed that I let him in. It was like déjà vu. He immediately put the gun to my face and asked me if I slept with the guy I had been dating. Apparently, the rumor was that I had but he did not even give me a chance to respond. In my mind it was truly none of his business anyway, after all, he was married! He shoved me across the room and I was able to run away from him. I ran upstairs and locked the bedroom door. He was right behind me and broke the double doors down.

Suddenly, we heard someone enter my house. It was his wife. He put his gun away and ran downstairs. I yelled "get the hell out of my house" but moments later, they both came upstairs. I could not believe he let her in. I just stood there cold as ice. He ordered his wife to sit on my bed while he continued to give me the third degree on how intimate I got with this other guy. I was so humiliated. It was surreal to me. Apparently my neighbors called the police because they arrived to diffuse the situation. They made his wife leave and asked me to step outside, away from Tom. Although they seemed to have a look as if I got what I deserved, they asked me if he was armed and whether I felt my life was in danger. I promptly told them "No, everything is okay." After filing a police report they pulled off and Tom left.

The next thing I knew my name was dirt. I heard that I was being called a slut, a cheater, a low-life, you name it, for what I did to Tom. What?! He was the victim? He was married and I was the cheater? It did not make sense.

My self-esteem was obliterated. I simply wanted out of it all. I did not know who to turn to or what to do to try to feel better. I was officially in a depression.

Up to that point in my life I had never had a drink alone but this particular night, I decided to have one. One turned into a whole bottle of wine and I got wasted. I also smoked around ten cigarettes just to take the self-deprecation one step further. I called my sister and told her that I was ready to die. Before I knew it I was telling the story of how Tom put a gun to my face and that he let his wife in my house and how I had been stalked by both of them for the past six months. It all came out. I couldn't stop divulging the information I had been ashamed to tell anyone for so long. My sister cried with me and told me how this world would not be complete without me in it. She filled me with love that night.

The next day, I was seeing clearly. The sun was shining bright. All the madness had come to a screeching halt because I was done. I had hit rock bottom and the only direction for me to go from there, was up.

TIME

*D*id this story surprise you? Or was this story about you, or one of your friends, at some point in your life? While the details of the story may be different, the lessons learned may be the same for many of us. There are many powerful points to draw from this experience.

For starters, what I did not realize is that you take yourself with you, wherever you go. Moving to another state or starting a new job, without doing the inner work would not forward me in making healthy choices in my life. I did not think highly of myself then. Do you remember what we said happens when we do not feel good about ourselves? Yes, we operate with gaps! And what did I immediately choose to fill my gaps? A married man. In retrospect, a clear sign that I was not making choices that served my highest good.

I also got swept up in what appeared good rather than what was actually good for me. I took pleasure in the non-stop social scene, the surprises and all of the attention but never experienced joy. I could not achieve joy when it all stemmed from the dishonest relationship I had to be in, in order to have it. I was too ashamed of myself and felt too bad about myself. Those enjoyable things simply served as band-aids for my boo-boos, if you will. The boo-boos being gaps. What I was really in search of was self-love but I could not make that distinction with all the chaos going on in my life.

How about when I chose to let Tom in my house when he was

clearly not being rational? I was willing to put myself in harm's way to avoid having my neighbors, whom I barely knew, think negatively of me. I made up that they would think I was weak, desperate, loose or pathetic. Back then I internalized what people thought of me so much that I found the idea of that more painful than the repercussions of Tom's rage. All the while, my neighbors were simply concerned for my well being. Not only did they call the cops but they even came by the next day to see if I was okay. It never occurred to me that would be their reaction.

Another self-sabotaging move was when I decided to date someone new rather than sorting through the mess I was already in. I did not take the time to learn from the slew of lessons that would only make me stronger. I have learned that we can go on and on avoiding the signs – the signs to look within rather than turn to external people, things or experiences. Think of all the signs I had throughout the relationship with Tom. He was married and I chose to get in the relationship anyway. Rather than have some dignity and integrity, I chose to break up and get back together with him every other day. He pulled a gun on me and I chose not to tell the cops. I chose to let him and his wife stalk me for six months and live in fear. Eventually, some sign large enough to knock me over the head came along and I couldn't run any further. For me, it was the exploration of killing myself that turned me around. I was done with the drama and now I wanted to find out how I got to such a low point.

L O V E

*N*ow this story has a dramatic ending. I really hit rock bottom before I decided to turn things around for myself but sometimes it is simply a switch that turns on in a woman's head that makes her choose what is best for her. I call it the *light bulb phenomenon* because it is as if a light bulb clicks in a woman's head and says I do not want to live like this anymore! Rather than listening to the million times someone lets us know we are making a mistake or the zillion times we told ourselves, it is an inner awareness that this time I am done.

A woman in an abusive relationship can end up in the hospital on her death bed and with her next breath choose to go back to her abuser. A couple months later when one least expects it, her light-bulb clicks and she opts out of the relationship for good. Once she has gotten to this point she will do whatever it takes to ensure there is no going back. However, this does not guarantee that she will never get into another abusive relationship, it simply means she got out of this one. *Until she does the inner work required to love herself in a way that no one else can, she will remain open and available to making poor choices. And this is okay! You do not have to make yourself feel bad, stupid or incorrigible because you've made the same poor choice over and over again. This is how we grow and come to the healthy awareness that all we have to do is love ourselves in order to break out of such a cycle.* Think of it as learning to ride a bike. If you chose to ditch learning to ride a bike the first time you fell off and scraped your knee, would you know how to ride a bike today? I use this light analogy because it is extremely important for you to lighten up on yourself. You want to make sure you do not beat yourself up for making poor choices no matter how many times you have a repeat offense. That beating is self-inflicted and turns into guilt, self-loathing and only serves to make you feel worse about yourself.

Chapter 6

It's Too High To Get Over and Too Low To Get Under

"Coming out of the dark
I finally see the light now
It's shining on me
Coming out of the dark
I know the love that saved me"

- Coming Out of the Dark, Gloria Estefan

 M E A N

At this point, I had taken all that I could take. I no longer knew how to survive the life that I was living. I had been attacked, abused, used, raped, stalked, rejected, threatened, judged, taken for granted, all in my relationships with men. I had hit rock bottom and was determined to turn things around. I was through with the self-inflicted cycle of destruction. I wasn't exactly sure how I was going to move forward but I knew that I had crossed a very dangerous line. I was playing with fire and I had to make some changes. Sadly, even with knowing this, there was still a part of me that wanted to get right back into another relationship and hide from the inevitable. It was time for me to face my fears. I had run long enough. The time had come for me to look within.

I was clear that I could not be in an intimate relationship and do the inner work that was necessary for me to be happy. So I made a conscious decision not to get into any. I had to focus all of my attention on me. It felt a bit too self-involved since I was used to focusing on others but I did it anyway because it felt like a necessity.

Little did I know I was about to embark on a deep spiritual transformation that had me look at some difficult events in my life from a brand new set of eyes. In an attempt to cover all my bases, I decided to take action on my mind, body and soul. I felt like all interdependent parts would come together whole.

I started seeing a therapist. I wanted an expert to help me understand and heal from my past. I boosted up my exercise routine significantly. I even started training for a half-marathon. Running helped me clear my mind. I started a vegan diet and ate only organic, pure foods. This not only made my body feel lighter but combined with the exercise my energy was through the roof. Most importantly I stepped into a church for the first time. Two of my friends had been inviting me to their church for months and I finally said yes.

At the first Sunday service I attended, I was nervous, scared and had no clue what to expect. I walked in the chapel and felt like everyone was watching me. As soon as we found our seats, I took a deep breath and the choir began to sing. Suddenly I felt this chill travel through my entire body from head to toe. I stood up and looked at the beautiful stained glass ceiling and began to cry. I opened my hands and raised them up as if to receive this presence that I could literally feel running through me. It was like nothing I had ever experienced before yet it felt familiar. It felt like pure, unconditional love moving in and through me. It was like being welcomed home exactly as I was. I kept whispering "I'm so sorry it took me so long, I'm so sorry it took me so long," as tears rolled down my cheeks. All of a sudden it did not matter if people noticed me stumble when we were asked to sit or stand. Or when I didn't know what a hymnal was and where to find one. Or when I mouthed the words to the *Lord's Prayer* because I didn't know it. It all didn't matter; I was clear why I was there. A conscious acknowledgement of God in my life had begun and it felt too good to let anything get in my way of nourishing that kind of love.

TIME

*T*his was the turnaround point of my life. I finally chose to look within, in a committed way. And out of that commitment, I created the right and perfect conditions for me to discover things about myself. Through eating well, exercising, processing my past and stepping into my spiritual awareness, I literally obliterated the ugly opinion of myself that had been influencing my life. Everything I discovered about myself became permanently embedded into my awareness causing constant triggers and reminders about who I am. From this point forward, even if I did something reminiscent of my past like something self-sabotaging or deprecating, I quickly modified my behavior based on the knowing that I am a spiritual being experiencing a spiritual evolution, capable of unconditional love and of being loved just as I am. When it comes down to it, this is who I am authentically! Loving and expressing my authentic self had been set into motion.

LOVE

A roller coaster has a series of high and low points on its path as does life. *Experiencing ups and downs is an inevitable consequence of living, but it is who we become during these ups and downs that will dictate our ability to stay the course of the spiritual, joyful and purposeful life that was meant for us to live.* You see, the circumstances or events may be beyond our control, but how much we love and express ourselves through these times is not! If we are not in this awareness, then we can lose sight of our divinity, or perfection, as a result of the ups and downs in our lives. We tend to let the experiences get bigger than us and let these experiences define or mold us. When you do that, you lose your authenticity. It gets lost in misperceptions until you begin to manifest behaviors that are not in alignment with who you are. I call this the *roller coaster effect.*

Have you ever been swept up in the highs of life so much that you lost touch with who you are? The best example I can give you is one I think many women can relate to. It is when you first fall in love. You feel so wonderful about yourself and it is like you are on a high that you cannot come down from. We kind of lose it don't we? Some women downplay their success because it makes their partner feel better. Some women wear sexier clothes or more makeup because it is their partner's preference. Some women permanently alter their bodies because it is what their partner likes.

How about when we put our friends and family on the back burner to a point where we find ourselves by ourselves when we come off the high? Most of my closest girlfriends live in another state than I, so our relationships are mostly nourished by phone. I can tell when they have a new man in their life, are reunited with their man or are experiencing a breakup, by the sharp decrease or increase in communication we share. During the breakups, we speak everyday and during the honeymoon or reunited stages they are really tough to connect with. I am fully aware that before I became a mother, I was the same way. Once a mother it is simply more difficult to spend quality time on the phone everyday, as making calls becomes very tricky especially during the early stages. Children hollering "Mommy" in the background, which many of you know is automatic as soon as they see you even go near the phone, is not conducive to an effective conversation. Okay I have digressed. Allow me to get back on track. It is completely logical that a woman has less time to spend with others because they are physically in the presence of this new love interest. It is when a woman is sacrificing other great relationships in her life for the sake of being with that person, that it becomes detrimental. If you have friendships that mean something to you, it is possible to make sure they stay meaningful friendships. You do not have to let the relationships suffer to the point where you lose them or have to ask for forgiveness because of your neglect.

The same holds true for things that you loved to do prior to entering into the new relationship. If you still love doing them, how about making the time to do them independently because you have chosen to and not because you managed to etch out some time while your intimate partner is not around or because you got their approval to do so? It is often the case that I hear a woman say, "My boyfriend or husband said I could go, so I did" or something of that nature. It is as if that approval is a necessary step in the process of doing something that you desire to do when really all that is necessary is for the two people in an intimate relationship to have a mutual respect for their individuality. It is from there that both people can be themselves without feeling like approval is necessary.

While a certain amount of adjustment and compromise is natural as two people come together in relationship, it is when we compromise our own core morals, values, spirituality, dignity and integrity that we leave ourselves open to sabotaging our self-esteem.

I have already spent a lot of time demonstrating how the lows in life can impact us so I will move on to discussing how our feelings relate to our authentic self.

When you feel good about yourself, you make choices that serve your highest good – your *true desires*. A true desire is a person, experience or thing you authentically draw into your life because they are in alignment with the core of who you are. When you feel bad about yourself, you make poor choices – choices that serve a *perceived need*. A perceived need is defined as a person, experience or thing you draw into your life because you think you need it.

True desires are supplementary to your life while perceived needs are complementary. This means that true desires add to your perfect, whole and complete self. You are engaging the true desires simply because you love to. *Perceived needs are those people, experiences or things that you choose so that you feel perfect, whole and complete when you do not actually deem yourself so.* These are the fillers that we symbolically embed into us, to make us feel whole. You are engaging the perceived needs because you think you cannot do without them.

The toggle between feelings and their resulting choices takes a toll on our lives if we let it. I have developed a term that I use to describe being your authentic self at all times despite what you are going through, what you may feel at any given moment of time or what someone else thinks of you. I call it your *"mean."* When you are fully accepting and loving of yourself no matter what, you are operating from your mean.

I must admit my engineering background led me to this insight because the mathematical definition of a mean is the average of two or more numbers. A mean always exists, it is a constant entity that takes into account all of the numbers it represents, even the extremes. All the points above the average and all those below it.

I draw a parallel where the numbers represent the highs and lows of life and the *mean represents BEING and LOVING your authentic self regardless of the circumstances, your past or how others perceive you.* You can break through the roller coaster effect by operating from your mean! By growing through the lows and simply experiencing the highs, you will achieve your mean and if you happen to veer off, like in a weak moment, you will get back to it because it is constant.

With each relationship in my past, I managed to get deeper and deeper into a low – further and further away from my mean. The problem was that I only knew bits and pieces of my authentic self. I chose to avoid getting to know myself and it was easiest to do so by focusing my attention on relationships. As I shared earlier, rather than learning about myself I was busy draining the love out of my partners in lieu of self-love. As a result, I could not love and express my authentic self because I was unknowingly out of alignment with who I am. I was caught in the flux of the ups and downs rather than living from my mean. However, I can guarantee that once you tap into your mean, you will never lose the flow of it and the peace that comes from knowing this will build confidence in your ability to address any situation that comes your way.

Chapter 7

You're One Choice Away From Self-Love

" Love
Be Encouraged
Love
It will see you through
Love
Be the first to
Love
Fill your heart with
Love"

- The Love Song, A song by Rickie Byars Beckwith

I was out to dinner with a guy I had been dating for a couple of weeks. The table at the restaurant had a paper table cloth and there were crayons available to us if we wanted to write on it. After a couple rounds of tic tac toe, we got on the conversation of relationships. We were discussing our beliefs and I remember telling him that I reached a point in my life where no person or thing could jolt me from being and loving myself. I continued to tell him that I had been through a lot in my lifetime but that "No matter what, I was going to be alright." When he asked me how I was so sure of that, I grabbed a crayon and proceeded to draw a schematic of a line graph with several high and low points along it. Then I drew a straight line through the center of the peaks and valleys to represent an average or a "mean" of those points along the line. I continued by explaining that I have a "mean". My mean represents loving myself so fully that even though I cared for him very much, if we were to break up I would feel sad, and let myself heal, but I would not tailspin into a world of low self-esteem and self-deprecation. That was no longer how I chose to be. I loved myself so much that the love anyone gave me was supplementary. It added to the love I had for myself. So if it was taken away for some reason, I was left with all my love and not one bit less! He was blown away by my explanation and we got a little bit closer that day.

W henever I share the *mean* concept, inevitably I will get some version of the question "Well how do I get to this nirvana place of total self acceptance, authenticity and self-love? This 'mean' you are talking about." While I can give you some very practical ideas to get there and I will, it is important to understand the inner workings of how to achieve your mean.

LOVE

*T*he first insight I'll share is, *fill your own gaps!* And in order to fill gaps, you must be cognizant of whether you are operating with them in your life. You will need to reflect on the choices you are making in your life. Making poor choices is a clear indication that you are operating with gaps. Here are some questions to ask yourself when exploring whether a choice is serving you or not:

- What is this choice creating in my life?
- How does it feel?
- Is it healthy?
- How is it serving me?
- How is it serving my loved ones?

If you take the time to answers these questions, even write the answers down, pray on them, meditate on them, whatever re-flective process works for you, you will become aware of how a choice has or will impact you.

Have you ever met a person who complains about their marriage all the time but says they are staying in it for the sake of their children? This is a perfect example of a choice that requires at-tention. Many people believe that it is best for children to have both their parents at home. But what if the parents are abu-sive, argumentative, indifferent or inauthentic with each other? Does this set a good example for their children? Definitely not. It paints a distorted picture of what a child may perceive as a healthy relationship. There is the possibility that the children will find themselves in very similar relationships when they grow up because it is primarily what they have been exposed to. So the bottom line is this choice must be cross-examined to determine if the person is filling gaps and has made up a really great excuse to do so, or if in fact staying in the marriage is truly best for their children.

Now for the second insight, choose to know that you are perfect, whole and complete at all times, in any situations and under all circumstances! Know that you do not need anyone or anything to be filled with love. You can attain self-love simply by choosing it. If you have the power to choose everything else in your life, why not choose this? Most people don't realize that it is an everyday choice to love yourself. In other words, with every new moment in your life, whether it appears to be a positive or a negative one, you can choose to love yourself. And if you haven't been doing this already, what you will start to see is a shift in your life. A shift from choices that are serving perceived needs to those that are in alignment with true desires and your authentic self.

The major challenge I have encountered in the work I do is that many women do not find it easy to choose empowering beliefs about themselves such as being perfect, whole and complete or being lovable, beautiful or strong. Many women have become so disheartened by what they have been through or what others think about them, that they are more comfortable believing negative thoughts. Perhaps, they do not want to be hurt or disappointed anymore but eventually behavior leads to a point where they simply do not believe anything positive about themselves. Often to the point where they won't even accept compliments from others.

A young lady once landed in one of my workshops and prominently declared that she did not trust anyone in her life and was absolutely happy that way. I asked her if she considered herself a trusting person, she was quick to say no. And when asked to share something that was holding her back in life, she said "everything is going well and I have no problems." I knew that she was not being honest and that there was a deep dark secret she was desperately craving to release. My next question to her was "do you consider yourself to be an honest person?" She paused to think about that one but did not answer. I said to her that despite her past she could simply choose that day to be trusting and honest by sharing something that she had never shared with anyone. Not because everyone in the group assured her that they were trustworthy but simply because she chose to. I went on to tell her that if she let out whatever it was, that she would feel much better afterwards. She had such a hard time grasping that concept and was so fearful of trusting the people in the room, that she argued her case for 'not trusting people' until finally she just sat down.

Towards the end of the workshop after everyone got up and spoke of what is holding them back in their lives, she began to cry uncontrollably. I asked her if she was ready to share. The young lady walked up to the front of the room and told us that she had been raped by her stepfather and that when she told her mother, her mother did not believe her. Then she got into a sexual relationship at a very young age with a guy that was unfaithful and physically abusive with her for years. After about fifteen minutes of sharing from the depths of her being, one traumatic experience after the other, she finally exhaled. She had never felt so free in her life. Not only did she choose to release all this pain that she was holding in for so long, she was able to trust! Not one person but about twenty-five! We still communicate regularly and she is thriving in her career and social life. And because she has learned to be trusting and honest with others, she receives it in return. However, when she is not trusted, it does not throw her from her mean.

Here is the key that can shift your perspective about yourself: It will serve you to realize that if you are capable of giving love, trust, compassion, honesty, authenticity, then you are capable of receiving them! In other words, if you ARE loving, trusting, compassionate, honest and authentic then you will attract those very same attributes in your life! *This is why I always encourage people to give of themselves without expectations! Give of yourself because it is simply who you are, the way you are and how you choose to be!* You do not have control over how other people will be with you but you do have control over who you choose to be at any given moment. This gets tougher when faced with adversity which is why it is very important to be grounded in who you are. Sometimes women simply need to fall in love with themselves before they can get to this solid ground. It entails getting to know you.

Women take on a lot of roles in life. We are mothers, daughters, sisters, lovers, caretakers, therapists, professionals and much more. These roles give us information about the type of person we are but they are not who we are. We spent some time clarifying your core essence which is identified by your morals, your values, your spirituality, your dignity and your integrity. When I ask women who they are in this context, many times they struggle to answer. Not necessarily because they don't know these things about themselves but because they are not able to articulate it. For the rest of them, it is because they have not taken the time to examine these dimensions of themselves. *Either way, we need to have this information about ourselves downloaded into our hearts, imprinted on our souls and reflected through our bodies. We need to be crystal clear so that when anyone, anything or any experience comes into our lives, the ways of being that are inherent to ourselves automatically flow out.*

It is easy to get engulfed in the day to day activities so it is imperative that you take the time to get to know you. *Not only will you gain confidence by knowing more about yourself and your capabilities, but the bonus is that you get clear on how amazing you truly are!* I offer the following ideas to support you in this journey of self-exploration and self-love, all to be done by *yourself:*

- Create a book with five chapters entitled: Morals, Values, Spirituality, Dignity and Integrity. Start off by writing in each chapter what you know about yourself in each respective chapter and continue to journal as you discover more about yourself.

- Spend at least one hour a day with no distractions that work your mind or body like people, television, books, exercise, food, driving or shopping. In other words, this is to be a separate hour outside of your normal routine. Use this time to engage your soul.

These days, I cherish every moment I have to myself. It is quite rare with a husband and two daughters. I remember when my first born learned to say "Mama" and it was her favorite word (and it still is today). I would stow away for fifteen minutes just to take a shower while my husband watched her. As I listened to the water falling and tuned out the "Mama, mama, mama..." repeating in the background, it was like I was having a 'Very Important Person' party and the celebration was for me!

- Go on a week long vacation to a location you have never been.

- Have dinner at a five star restaurant.

- Go to the movies.

- Host a picnic in the park.

🐢 Pick a minimum of two causes that you are passionate about and volunteer your time to them.

🐢 Start a conversation with a complete stranger about who you are (as defined by your Morals, Values, Spirituality, Dignity and Integrity) and encourage them to share who they are with you.

🐢 Turn a difficult situation in your life into a positive one no matter how scary it may be. Discover who it required you to *be* to do so. What *ways of being* did you access to have this occur?

🐢 Release painful experiences that may be holding you back from expressing your true self. This may require a form of support like a therapist, personal development workshop/ training or life coach.

Chapter 8

Get Your Life Off Cruise Control!

"When I dream
I dream in color
I want to love
Not just a lover"

- Dream in Color, A song by Regina Belle

 M E A N

I was just getting home from my final therapy session followed by a nice long run. While I always felt the therapy sessions went well, I found the running far more therapeutic. Nonetheless, having an impartial person to speak to about some of the painful events of my life did help. We spent a lot of time analyzing my childhood through teenage years and the time I was raped. My psychiatrist felt it was essential that I understand my feelings from these periods of my life in order to move forward.

95

What came up for me was that I made a lot of mistakes during my teenage years. I had succumbed to peer pressure. I spent lots of time partying instead of focusing on school. I joined in with other kids that were heavy into smoking cigarettes and drinking alcohol. I would stay out until very late hours, if I even came home at all, leaving myself vulnerable to dangerous situations. And dangerous situations are exactly what happened. I dug so deep that things I had forgotten about were coming up. I remembered the time when I was fifteen years old and got drunk at a club. An older man that I didn't know managed to lure me away from my friends. Three hours later my friends found me in the women's bathroom while the guy was kissing on my neck. They grabbed me away from the man and took me home. Two things came to mind as I recollected this experience. I immediately expressed gratitude that it did not end up worse like being raped, kidnapped or killed.

The other thought was that club owners would sell their souls to make more money. They let pretty little girls into their venues despite the law, and put them in harm's way, just so that they can make money. They know that where there are cute girls, the guys that buy them drinks will come. Basically, I was used by these club owners for my sex appeal even though I barely even knew what sex appeal meant! At the time, I just thought it was cool that the bouncer would bring me and my friends to the front of the line and let us into the club like VIP. It sickened me to know that I put myself in that situation among many others equally as detrimental. Even when I was raped, I was on a date that I chose to go on! While the violence was unexpected and by no means did I deserve it, I couldn't ignore the fact that I put myself there to receive it.

It was great to have these insights but now where did I go with them. Why was I still making poor choices in my life? The therapy sessions may have been over but I was definitely not through with the healing process.

One day while on an eleven mile run, I had an epiphany. I figured out that I had been letting my past mistakes make me feel guilty and inept. And these feelings were influencing how I navigated through life. It made perfect sense. How could I make good choices in my life if what I really believed is that I was incapable of doing so? I did not believe in or love myself enough to know that I was in fact fully capable. I was ready to release myself from the stronghold of my past. I had no desire to continue feeling bad about myself or making bad choices, when I had no power to go back and change things.

I decided to write a list of all the mistakes I believed I made so I could get it all into perspective. At this point it did not matter why I made the mistakes I just wanted to purge myself of them. I also made a list of all the people who did something hurtful to me including the rapist and the older man from the club. As I recounted these events I felt a great sense of relief. I was no longer harboring any pain. I was able to recollect these events without feeling hurt, damaged or scared. Now if I could get rid of the self-inflicted guilt, I would be all set.

I decided to do something silly. I was going to look myself in the mirror and tell myself that I am forgiven for all the mistakes I made. And then I was going to take a picture of a random person from a magazine and use it in place of all the people that had hurt me. One by one, I forgave myself and others for all the painful events of my past. Admittedly, at the start I really did feel silly but as I connected with what I was actually doing, I started to cry. I got really emotional. I literally felt the guilt and shame leave my mind, body and soul. I had no idea how something so simple could be so powerful. From that point forward,

I was free from the influence of my past. I could objectively reference my past without internalizing any negative feelings that may come up. Going forward, anytime I made a poor choice, I went through the same exact process to release myself of any known or unknown influences.

Reflecting on this liberating time of my life, I recognize two things had come together enabling me to release the chokehold of my past. My desire to detach myself from self-inflicted pain met up my desire to approach each new moment with innovation and zeal. I was tired of all the pain I was harboring that had been influencing how I approached my life. I was ready to move forward. If I had not been committed to letting go of my past, I could have gone through the motions of that forgiveness exercise over and over again and end up with no sense of freedom. But I was perfectly primed to discover the power of forgiveness and the gift of each new moment.

L O V E

You have the opportunity to access any ways of being you wish to express with each new moment. Each moment is a new opportunity to choose someone or something new. You are not obligated to seek evidence from the past that will support you in how to be in the present moment. In fact, it is essential that you do *not* refer to the past in order to be yourself authentically. You must do your best to look beyond "what you know." If you stay within what you know, then you become stagnant. You hinder your growth and block new people, experiences and things from coming into your life. Admittedly, this is a safe "go to" for people. If a woman has been hurt by an intimate partner in the past, she may hesitate to be intimate with someone again. If a woman trusted someone and was betrayed by that person, she may not choose to trust again. If a woman went for her dream and gave up because of a bad experience, she may never choose to go for it again. If a woman breaks up with her boyfriend and does not like feeling alone afterwards, she may go back to him even though he is not the one for her. Our past has the ability to prevent us from making choices that serve our highest good.

New and uncharted possibilities can seem scary and feel uncomfortable. I cannot count how many times I have asked women how a new experience felt and the answer was "It felt uncomfortable." But right after they say it, they explain all the good that came from that very experience. It is uncomfortable because in that moment, you are growing and learning new things. You are forced to rely on being yourself in that moment, rather than some previous version of yourself. I often say, it is outside of your comfort zone where all the magic happens!

FORGIVENESS

Another key to living in the moment is forgiveness. *Forgiveness liberates you from your past. When you withhold forgiveness, what you are really doing is holding on to destructive feelings.* Therefore, you are being guided by your feelings and you are holding yourself out of alignment with your authentic self. In other words, you are not operating at your mean.

There are two common pitfalls that relate to forgiveness. One is that people think forgiveness is for other people when in fact forgiveness is for none other than yourself! By definition, withholding forgiveness is fostering destructive feelings which are unhealthy. There are people that believe withholding forgiveness has the ability to create health issues, diseases and disorders. Whether you believe that or not, at a minimum it does cause stress. Stress can develop in your body with you being none the wiser and it manifests through the body in a plethora of ways ranging from small ailments to very serious ones. Withholding forgiveness does equal damage to you emotionally as it does physically. So it is in your best interest to release it and forgive.

The other pitfall is that people do not realize the significance of forgiving themselves. Partially because they don't know how to, but mostly because it does not occur to them to do so. We tend to focus on what others did to us but remember that if we look at choices from an empowering view, then we know that we have done things to ourselves that do not serve our highest good. Further, if we have ever operated with gaps, then we know we have made choices that were detrimental to us and caused us to pay prices. If we fail to see the importance of forgiving ourselves, we can go on hosting destructive feelings for a very long time preventing us from being authentic.

So in order to gain this freedom to be yourself in the moment, you want to forgive yourself for all the poor choices you have made, forgive yourself for any negative experiences you have been through and forgive those who have brought you pain.

When working with forgiveness, there are a few cardinal rules:

1. *You must make the choice to forgive.*

2. *You must do the work required to fully heal from the situation before you can forgive.* Don't simply forgive because you know it will help you move forward. If you are not ready, you will quickly learn that you are not over it yet. Someday when it comes up again you will find that you still have some negative energy around it. You will get a signal that may look or feel like tears, anger, frustration, regret, guilt or hopelessness. Has one of your girlfriends ever tried to convince you that she is over her ex-boyfriend that broke up with her but as she is presenting her case you start to see her body language, behavior and tone of voice tell a completely different story? She gives you clear signs that she is not over him yet. It's because she has not taken the time to heal from the breakup.

3. *Once you have made the choice to forgive and have healed, you must release it in person or symbolically.* The actual activity of forgiveness partners with the choice you have made to forgive and allows for the actual release. Have you ever felt better after blurting out a secret you have been yearning to share for a long time? It is because you are physically releasing something that you really wanted

to let out. Well the same holds for forgiveness. You need to physically let it out of your system. When forgiving a person, it can be powerful to do it in person. However, sometimes the person is long gone from your life, deceased or it is unadvisable to seek them out.

Some ideas to symbolically forgive are:

- Put a chair in front of a full length mirror. Connect with yourself by maintaining strong and powerful eye contact throughout the forgiveness process. When ready, express to your reflection what you are forgiving yourself or others for and verbalize your forgiveness. "I forgive myself for..." or "I forgive Jane Doe for..." Continue until nothing more comes to your heart.

- Role play where someone represents the person or experience you are seeking to forgive. Establish strong and powerful eye contact and do not lose it throughout the forgiveness process. When ready, express to them what you are forgiving them for and verbalize your forgiveness.

- Write a letter to yourself, the person or experience expressing what you are forgiving and your forgiveness. Do not send it, instead burn it or bury it to signify that the withholding no longer exists.

- Write a poem that symbolically expresses what you are forgiving and your forgiveness of it. Frame it and set it somewhere that will remind you that you have forgiven yourself, the person or experience.

Be diligent in taking these steps so that you can leave past guilt, self-loathing and negative influences behind so that you are free to be yourself in every new moment.

Chapter 9

Check Your Feelings at the Door

"I break tradition, sometimes my tries, are outside the lines. We've been conditioned to not make mistakes, but I can't live that way. Staring at the blank page before you. Open up the dirty window. Let the sun illuminate the words that you could not find. Reaching for something in the distance. So close you can almost taste it. Release your inhibitions. Feel the rain on your skin. No one else can feel it for you"

- Unwritten, A song by Natasha Bedingfield

MEAN

I was miserable at my job. Everyday was the same routine. I drove to work, half the time unconsciously, got to my cubicle, read my email and then tackled whatever projects I was assigned to. I thought to myself each and every morning, "when am I going to get out of here?" I remembered when the

type of work I did was remotely fun. I was an engineering ana-
lyst and had been in the field, in some form or fashion, for about
eight years. Although I was great at what I did, I felt no passion
anymore. The thrill was completely gone. I was craving more.
One of the exciting things going on in my life was a business
endeavor that I was working on with a very close friend of mine.
We had built a consulting business from scratch and after two
years of establishing a foundation, it was finally starting to take
off. My friend had recently left her job to work full time on
sales with the intention of creating enough revenue for both
of us to eventually be salaried full time. It was risky especially
since we essentially did not have enough revenue for either of
us to be paid a salary but my friend was determined to make it
happen. While the actual work was very similar to what I was
doing at my job, I felt more freedom and pride in what I was
doing with my consulting firm.

It was a lot of work. We had to handle sales, marketing, strategy,
finances, technology and most importantly the end product or
service for our clients. I was dedicated and spent many hours after a full work day dedicated to the business. At times I felt like
superwoman and was impressed by how I did it all. Especially
since, by this time I had also started a non-profit organization,
with my boyfriend, aimed at empowering teenagers to live their
dreams. I was passionate about helping girls break through self-
esteem issues and this was the perfect forum to do so. Even
though I put in a lot of effort to make the camps happen, it
never once felt like work for me. I was making a difference with
people and it felt good.

As I continued juggling all my commitments, something in me
kept resonating with this desire to help people. Sure the services
my consulting firm provided were helping businesses, and as a
result helping people, but I wanted to make more of a difference

– in a way that reached people at their heart and soul. I decided to ask my friend if we could have a strategy meeting about the values, mission and vision of our company. We often had these types of weekend long getaway meetings where we left behind the day to day happenings so that we could focus on such big concepts and of course have some fun. After all, we were not just business partners, we had a ten year relationship filled with girl talk, college memories, exotic travels, support in our various relationships, shoulders to cry on and all the wonderful things that make up a great friendship.

By the end of the weekend, I realized that we were not on the same page. I learned that our objectives for being in the business were different. I did not think that my purpose was more right than hers or vice versa but as I thought about some of our previous business decisions, I recognized that the difference caused us to make quite a few compromises. By compromising, each of us sacrificed a bit of our values so that we could move forward.

Soon after I had this realization, my boyfriend convinced me to take a personal development training that he thought would be a great experience for me. It was located out of state. I signed up for the course and bought my airline ticket.

The training was life changing and was the best thing that could have happened to me at that point in my life. The biggest lesson I learned was how to be authentic and how to be myself regardless of the circumstances, consequences or how it looks to other people. It seemed so simple a message but I was transformed – I was no longer capable of being inauthentic. My conscience would not allow it. As a result, there were some changes I needed to make in my life and while I felt it would be a huge relief to finally get real, I was concerned about rocking the boat too much.

First and foremost, I admitted to myself that I was not driven by passion in my consulting business but I was more driven by the desire to get out of the mundane routine of my job and having more freedom. Further, I acknowledged that my purpose is to help women break through low self-esteem issues. Finally, I became aware that there were relationships and friendships in my life that were not good for me yet I had been holding on to them for various reasons. I needed to address these realizations if I had any chance of being authentic.

My biggest dilemma was pulling out of the consulting business because I feared it would hurt my best friend. Even though she was what many would call a "tough cookie," I knew she wanted us to do this together. And since she was a strong woman with a personality to match, at times I found it intimidating. I had to make sure that no matter how she reacted, I could remain loving because I truly had both of us in mind when making this choice. I wanted to focus on my purpose but I also did not want to drag the business down because of my lack of passion. The conversation went worse than I could have imagined. We got into a huge argument in the middle of a local Starbucks. For the next few weeks as we tried to produce work we were hired to do by a client, things were very strained. I kept bringing up the topic of parting ways on our venture but it never ended up in a good way. She simply could not see the positives of my decision. Admittedly, it had to be tough for her to do so when she had recently left the security of a full time job and was basically counting on us to make it together. Her solution to the dissolution of our partnership was to hire a lawyer to draft the contract and negotiate a settlement. I found it so impersonal and was hurt by this tactic but I went along with it. We even ended up in a screaming match in front of the lawyer. From that point forward, our friendship had whittled down to nothing. Both of us were angry and hurting but I could not help but know that

I was making the right choice for the both of us. After all, it stemmed from authenticity and nowhere else.

I went on to realize my dream of writing an inspirational book for women, growing my non-profit youth organization and launching my workshops to empower women. My partner grew the consulting business to a six figure revenue grossing company within a year.

A year later, on my wedding day, I had nine bridesmaids that I called amazing friends and was surrounded by people I loved and who loved me. A few months after the wedding, I called my partner to apologize for the way things turned out. Today, we are friends again. We do not get to spend a whole lot of time together or even speak very often but we certainly love each other.

I M E

*I*s that powerful or what? When I got clear on who I am, I moved in the direction of my purpose and passion despite how hard I had to rock the boat and it turned out amazingly! I remember going through a gamut of feelings: fear, happiness, excitement, anxiety, doubt, sadness, anger. I had my own mini-roller coaster going. *But what I learned was that we must let ourselves feel but not be guided by our feelings. In other words, process your feelings, heal from them if necessary, let them run their course but do not take action until you have become grounded in your authentic self.* It is from there that you make the choices that serve you. Even if it does not look like it at the time, like having screaming matches, losing a friend or losing financial security. Hold tight! As long as you are clear that you have made this choice authentically, the good is coming!

LOVE

With each new moment you are given, you have the opportunity to love yourself so fully that you are compelled to stay true to yourself. *Equally important to knowing who you are is freely expressing it in all situations no matter how difficult it may seem.* Every time you withhold your authentic self, you move out of alignment with the core of who you are which leaves you susceptible to making choices that do not serve your highest good.

In addition, every time you are inauthentic, you hand your power over to another person or thing. In other words, that person or thing has the power to impact who you are being, – your feelings, attitude and behavior – in that moment. A common example of this is reacting on impulse. Have you ever been honked or yelled at by another driver on the road and retaliated by yelling back or addressing them with a particular hand gesture? In that moment this person had the power to make you angry which prompted you to react this way. Perhaps if you took time to get grounded by taking a deep breath and counting to five, you may find a way to be that is more in alignment with who you are. For example, you may have realized that this person is hurting and that is why she is lashing out at people on the road. This may have changed your reaction from one of anger and retaliation to a new response that is caring, understanding or compassionate because that is who you are. Reaction can be difficult to overcome because sometimes it is knee-jerk but if you think about the fact that there are limitless ways to react to a situation you may find that it isn't an insurmountable challenge. However, it may require you to *shift* from whatever feelings you have in the moment so that you are able to *respond* rather than *react*. Let's go back to our example. Another response other than yelling at the hostile driver could have been to simply move out of their way. You could have taken their license plate to report them which may sound unkind but could actually serve them depending on their level of road rage. Another response would be to wish them a wonderful day. You could pray for them or virtually give them words of encouragement. You could have apologized for whatever you did that made them upset. You could have smiled at them and went on your merry way. I could go on but I think you get the point, which is that someone else's reaction to you does not have to impact how your authentic self would respond. It just may require you to shift first. It's okay to be angry, however, we want to let ourselves feel and not be guided by or take action based on our feelings. The sooner we 'get off it' or shift, the sooner we get back to our authentic selves.

SHIFTING

Shifting is a powerful tool that supports being authentic no matter what situations come our way. It requires you to take time to intentionally get over your feelings so that you are not influenced by them. Have you ever been in an argument with your loved one and it lasts so long that you find yourself missing them? By day two of not speaking to each other you have something you really want to share with them but you choose to withhold because of the argument? Well I sure have. I have gone up to three days without speaking to my husband in the name of "being mad" rather than being authentic. Meanwhile my true desire is to have open lines of communication with him at all times because he is the first person I run to when I want to share something that happens in my life. By using the technique of shifting, I am able to significantly cut down the time I spend being inauthentic. Rather, I focus on what really matters to me. Now, if I am unsuccessful at avoiding an argument by shifting, at least I am able to apologize for my behavior afterwards and express my concerns in a vulnerable, loving way. And by doing so, love inevitably comes into play creating an open space for both of us to express ourselves authentically.

Getting authentic requires a full examination of your life's state of affairs and then taking action. You look at the various domains of your life and determine whether what you have going on in each one is in alignment with the core of who you are. If it is not, then there is opportunity to get authentic. At a minimum the domains you want to look at are: Spirituality, Intimate Relationship, Family, Friendship, Career, Finances, Health, Community (Service) and Education. Here are some questions to support you in cross-examining the various aspects of these domains:

1. Am I experiencing more ups than downs? Do the advantages outweigh the disadvantages?

2. Am I fulfilled?
3. Am I joyful?
4. Am I dedicating the amount of time I wish to it?
5. Am I sharing my thoughts and beliefs?
6. Am I free to express myself?
7. Am I loved and accepted as I am?
8. Am I growing and evolving?
9. Am I diligent in my practices?
10. Am I giving and receiving?

If you say no to any of these questions, then that is where you want to take action, with the intention of getting authentic, in the respective domain.

Next you want to set the direction in which to take action. In other words, it is helpful to know what you are moving towards. You want to paint the picture of how an authentic life looks for you. You can do this by articulating all of your true desires within the context of these primary domains we just examined. This will act as a guide or a roadmap to the life of your dreams.

AN EXERCISE IN GETTING CLEAR

I have designed the following worksheets to support you in 'painting the picture' of your dream life. You will essentially answer Who, What, Where, When and Why for all of the domains of your life. First, I ask that you complete each worksheet for your current state of affairs, where applicable. For example, if you do not currently have a career, then skip that one. After you have completed all of them describing how your life is now,

I want you to take a break so that you can approach the second half of the exercise refreshed and renewed. Do whatever it takes to recharge so that you have released *all* feelings about your current state and get grounded in authenticity.

Next, you want to answer these questions about your authentic state of affairs which we will call the life of your dreams! Approach these questions without any influences from your current situation even if there are similarities, still go through the entire process. You want to describe your dream life as big, as powerful and as detailed as you can! So much that you can practically taste it! Keep in mind that it is okay if you cannot answer all of the questions right now because your true desires evolve as you do. Just be diligent about revisiting this exercise as you gain new insights. It would be great to do this exercise in your journal but if you do not have one, do it somewhere that is easily accessible to you.

CURRENT STATE OF AFFAIRS

Spirituality

* Use this worksheet to describe your *current* Spirituality.
* When answering each question be as descriptive as possible.
* Give plenty of examples.

What

What is your spirituality?
  a. How do you define your spirituality?
  b. How do you describe your spiritual journey?
What role does spirituality play in your life?
What are your spiritual practices?
What do you give to your spirituality?
What do you receive from your spirituality?

Why

Why is spirituality important to you?
  a. Is your spirituality in alignment with your authentic self? If so, how?
  b. Are you able to express yourself fully? If so, how?
  c. Are you passionate about your spirituality? If so, how do you know?
  d. Are your gifts, talents and skills being nourished? If so, how?

Who

Who supports you in your spiritual journey?
Who do you talk to about your spirituality?
Who is impacted by your spirituality?

Where

Where do you perform your spiritual practices?
  a. Are you in an environment where you can be open and receptive?
  b. Describe your surroundings.

When

When do you perform your spiritual practices?
  a. How much time per day do you dedicate to your spiritual practices?
  b. What time(s) of day do you practice?

Intimate Relationship

❋ Use this worksheet to describe your *current* Intimate Relationship.
❋ When answering each question be as descriptive as possible.
❋ Give plenty of examples.

Who

Who are you in this relationship with? Describe in context of their authentic self.
Who does this relationship impact?
Who supports you in this relationship?

Why

Why are you in this relationship?
   a. Do you love this person? If so, how do you know?
   b. Are you able to express yourself fully? If so, how?
   c. Are your gifts, talents and skills appreciated? If so, how?
   d. Are you passionate about this relationship?
      If so, how do you know?

What

What does your intimate partner look, feel, smell and sound like?
What types of things do you like to do together?
What types of things do you like to do apart?
What do you give to your intimate partner in this relationship?
What do you receive from your intimate partner in this relationship?

Where

Where are you in this relationship?
   a. Do you live close to your intimate partner or is it a long distance relationship?
   b. If you share the same home, what does it look, feel, smell and sound like?
   c. Do you have friends and/or family in your vicinity?

When

When do you see yourself in this relationship or are you currently in it?
When do you spend time with your intimate partner?
   a. How many hours a week do you spend with your intimate partner?
   b. How much time do you spend without your intimate partner (other than when you are at work)?
   c. How much time do you spend with family and friends?

Family

❋ Use this worksheet to describe your **current** Family.
❋ When answering each question be as descriptive as possible.
❋ Give plenty of examples.

Who

Who is your family? Desribe them.
a. How do you feel about them?
b. How do they feel about you?

Why

Why do you choose your family?
a. Do you love your family? If so, how do you know?
b. Are you able to express yourself fully with your family? If so, how?
c. Are your gifts, talents and skills appreciated? If so, how?
d. Are you passionate about your family? If so, how do you know?

What

What is the relationship with your family like?
a. How do you express your feelings to them?
b. How do they express their feelings to you?
What types of things do you like to do together?
What do you give to your family?
What do you receive from your family?

Where

Where is your family?
a. Do they live close by or far away? How do you feel about it?
b. Where do you enjoy being with them?

When

When do you spend time with your family?
a. How often do you see your family?

Frienship

* Use this worksheet to describe your *current* Friendships.
* When answering each question be as descriptive as possible.
* Give plenty of examples.

Who

Who are your friends? Describe them.
a. How do you feel about them?
b. How do they feel about you?

Why

Why are you friends with them?
a. Do you love your friends? If so, how do you know?
b. Are you able to express yourself fully? If so, how?
c. Are your gifts, talents and skills appreciated? If so, how?
d. Are you passionate about these friendships? If so, how do you know?

What

What is the relationship with your friends like?
a. How do you express your feelings to them?
b. How do they express their feelings to you?
What types of things do you like to do together?
What do you give to your friends?
What do you receive from your friends?

Where

Where are your friends? Do they live near you or far away?
Where do you spend time with them?

When

When do you spend time with your friends?
a. How often do you see you friends?

* Use this worksheet to describe your *current* Career.
* When answering each question be as descriptive as possible.
* Give plenty of examples.

What

What career do you want?
What does your career look like?
What are your day to day responsibilities and activities?
What is the greater purpose for your career?
What does your career feel like?
What do you give to this career?
What do you receive from this career?
What does the future hold for you in this career?

Why

Why have you chosen this career?
   a. Is it in alignment with your authentic self? If so, how?
   b. Are you able to express yourself fully? If so, how?
   c. Do you love your career? If so, how do you know?
   d. Are you passionate about your career? If so, how
      do you know?
   e. Are your gifts, talents and skills utilized? If so, how?

Who

Who do you get to be around in this career? Describe them.
Who does your career impact?
Who supports you in this career?

Where

Where is your career located?
   a. What state are you in?
   b. What is the weather like?
   c. What does it look like?
   d. How does it smell?
   e. Do you have friends and/or family in your vicinity?

When

When do you see yourself in this career or are
you currently in it?
When do you spend time working on your career?
   a. How many hours per week do you work?
   b. What is your weekly schedule?
   c. How much free time do you have?

Finances

- Use this worksheet to describe your ***current*** Finances.
- When answering each question be as descriptive as possible.
- Give plenty of examples.

What

What are your financial goals?
- a. What is your annual income?
- b. Do you own or rent a home?
- c. How much 'disposable' income do you have?
- d. What kind of lifetstyle do you have?

What does your home look, feel, smell and sound like?

Why

Why do you have these financial goals?
- a. Is your financial situation in alignment with your authentic self? If so, how?
- b. Does your financial situation support you in expressing yourself fully? If so, how?
- c. Are you happy with your financial situation? If so, how do you know?

Who

Who does your money impact?

Where

Where does your money go?
- a. What are your major expense categories?
- b. What are your necessities?
- c. What are your luxuries?
- d. How much do you give to charity?

When

When will you have this financial position or do you currently have it?

Health

* Use this worksheet to describe your *current* Health.
* When answering each question be as descriptive as possible.
* Give plenty of examples.

What

What is your general state of health?
What does your body feel like?
What does your body look like?
What does your mind feel like?
What actions do you take to tend to your body?
What is your exercise routine?
What are your eating habits?
What actions do you take to tend to your mind?
What, if any, are your health challenges?
a. How do you handle health challenges?

Why

Why is having good health important to you?
a. Is living a healthy lifestyle in alignment with your authentic self? If so, how?
b. Does being healthy support you in expressing yourself fully? If so, how?
c. Do you love your state of health?
e. Are you passionate about being healthy? If so, how do you know?

Who

Who does being healthy impact? And how does it impact them?
Who supports you in living a healthy lifestyle?

Where

Where do you take care of yourself?
a. Do you workout at home, outdoors or at a gym?
b. Are you in a conducive environment to think clearly?
c. Are you in a conducive environment for positive thinking?
d. Describe your environment.
e. Where do you eat healthy meals?

When

When do you spend time taking care of yourself?
a. How much time do you spend taking care of yourself?
b. What is your exercise schedule?
c. How much time do you spend selecting and preparing your meals?
d. How much time do you spend clearing your mind and thinking positive thoughts?

Community

* Use this worksheet to describe your *current* commitment to Community.
* When answering each question be as descriptive as possible.
* Give plenty of examples.

What

What do you do for your community?

Why

Why do you choose to make a difference in your community?
a. Is it in alignment with your authentic self? If so, how?
b. Are you able to express yourself fully? If so, how?
c. Are you passionate about the difference you make in your community? If so, how do you know?
d. Are you using your gifts, talents and skills? If so, how?

Who

Who is impacted by what you do in your community?

Where

Where do you make a difference in your community?

When

When do you spend time making a difference in your community?
a. How often do you do community work?

Education

* Use this worksheet to describe your *current* Education.
* When answering each question be as descriptive as possible.
* Give plenty of examples.

What

What do you want to learn?
What are your educational goals?
What do you give to your education?
What do you receive from your education?

Why

Why do you want to learn?
  a. How does it feel to learn?
  b. Does it support you in expressing yourself fully?
     If so, how?
  c. Are your gifts, talents and skills growing?
     If so, how?
  d. Are you passionate about learning?
     If so, how do you know?

Who

Who is impacted by your education?
Who supports you in your education?

Where

Where do you get your education?

When

When do you spend time getting your education?
  a. How much time do you spend learning?
  b. How often do you choose to learn?

⤳THE LIFE OF YOUR DREAMS

Spirituality

❋ Use this worksheet to describe your *dream* Spirituality.
❋ When answering each question be as descriptive as possible.
❋ Give plenty of examples.

What

What is your spirituality?
a. How do you define your spirituality?
b. How do you describe your spiritual journey?
What role does spirituality play in your life?
What are your spiritual practices?
What do you give to your spirituality?
What do you receive from your spirituality?

Why

Why is spirituality important to you?
a. Is your spirituality in alignment with your authentic self? If so, how?
b. Are you able to express yourself fully? If so, how?
c. Are you passionate about your spirituality? If so, how do you know?
d. Are your gifts, talents and skills being nourished? If so, how?

Who

Who supports you in your spiritual journey?
Who do you talk to about your spirituality?
Who is impacted by your spirituality?

Where

Where do you perform your spiritual practices?
a. Are you in an environment where you can be open and receptive?
b. Describe your surroundings.

When

When do you perform your spiritual practices?
a. How much time per day do you dedicate to your spiritual practices?
b. What time(s) of day do you practice?

Intimate Relationship

❊ Use this worksheet to describe your *dream* Intimate Relationship.
❊ When answering each question be as descriptive as possible.
❊ Give plenty of examples.

Who

Who are you in this relationship with? Describe in context of their authentic self.
Who does this relationship impact?
Who supports you in this relationship?

Why

Why are you in this relationship?
a. Do you love this person? If so, how do you know?
b. Are you able to express yourself fully? If so, how?
c. Are your gifts, talents and skills appreciated? If so, how?
d. Are you passionate about this relationship? If so, how do you know?

What

What does your intimate partner look, feel, smell and sound like?
What types of things do you like to do together?
What types of things do you like to do apart?
What do you give to your intimate partner in this relationship?
What do you receive from your intimate partner in this relationship?

Where

Where are you in this relationship?
a. Do you live close to your intimate partner or is it a long distance relationship?
b. If you share the same home, what does it look, feel, smell and sound like?
c. Do you have friends and/or family in your vicinity?

When

When do you see yourself in this relationship or are you currently in it?
When do you spend time with your intimate partner?
a. How many hours a week do you spend with your intimate partner?
b. How much time do you spend without your intimate partner (other than when you are at work)?
c. How much time do you spend with family and friends?

Family

❀ Use this worksheet to describe your **dream** Family.
❀ When answering each question be as descriptive as possible.
❀ Give plenty of examples.

Who

Who is your family? Desribe them.
  a. How do you feel about them?
  b. How do they feel about you?

Why

Why do you choose your family?
  a. Do you love your family? If so, how do you know?
  b. Are you able to express yourself fully with your family?
     If so, how?
  c. Are your gifts, talents and skills appreciated? If so, how?
  d. Are you passionate about your family? If so, how do you
     know?

What

What is the relationship with your family like?
  a. How do you express your feelings to them?
  b. How do they express their feelings to you?
What types of things do you like to do together?
What do you give to your family?
What do you receive from your family?

Where

Where is your family?
  a. Do they live close by or far away? How do you feel
     about it?
  b. Where do you enjoy being with them?

When

When do you spend time with your family?
  a. How often do you see your family?

Frienship

* Use this worksheet to describe your *dream* Friendships.
* When answering each question be as descriptive as possible.
* Give plenty of examples.

Who

Who are your friends? Describe them.
a. How do you feel about them?
b. How do they feel about you?

Why

Why are you friends with them?
a. Do you love your friends? If so, how do you know?
b. Are you able to express yourself fully? If so, how?
c. Are your gifts, talents and skills appreciated? If so, how?
d. Are you passionate about these friendships? If so, how do you know?

What

What is the relationship with your friends like?
a. How do you express your feelings to them?
b. How do they express their feelings to you?
What types of things do you like to do together?
What do you give to your friends?
What do you receive from your friends?

Where

Where are your friends? Do they live near you or far away?
Where do you spend time with them?

When

When do you spend time with your friends?
a. How often do you see you friends?

Career

* Use this worksheet to describe your *dream* Career.
* When answering each question be as descriptive as possible.
* Give plenty of examples.

What

What career do you want?
What does your career look like?
What are your day to day responsibilities and activities?
What is the greater purpose for your career?
What does your career feel like?
What do you give to this career?
What do you receive from this career?
What does the future hold for you in this career?

Why

Why have you chosen this career?
   a. Is it in alignment with your authentic self? If so, how?
   b. Are you able to express yourself fully? If so, how?
   c. Do you love your career? If so, how do you know?
   d. Are you passionate about your career? If so, how do you know?
   e. Are your gifts, talents and skills utilized? If so, how?

Who

Who do you get to be around in this career? Describe them.
Who does your career impact?
Who supports you in this career?

Where

Where is your career located?
   a. What state are you in?
   b. What is the weather like?
   c. What does it look like?
   d. How does it smell?
   e. Do you have friends and/or family in your vicinity?

When

When do you see yourself in this career or are you currently in it?
When do you spend time working on your career?
   a. How many hours per week do you work?
   b. What is your weekly schedule?
   c. How much free time do you have?

Finances

❋ Use this worksheet to describe your **dream** Finances.
❋ When answering each question be as descriptive as possible.
❋ Give plenty of examples.

What

What are your financial goals?
a. What is your annual income?
b. Do you own or rent a home?
c. How much 'disposable' income do you have?
d. What kind of lifetstyle do you have?
What does your home look, feel, smell and sound like?

Why

Why do you have these financial goals?
a. Is your financial situation in alignment with your authentic self? If so, how?
b. Does your financial situation support you in expressing yourself fully? If so, how?
c. Are you happy with your financial situation? If so, how do you know?

Who

Who does your money impact?

Where

Where does your money go?
a. What are your major expense categories?
b. What are your necessities?
c. What are your luxuries?
d. How much do you give to charity?

When

When will you have this financial position or do you currently have it?

Health

* Use this worksheet to describe your *dream* Health.
* When answering each question be as descriptive as possible.
* Give plenty of examples.

What

What is your general state of health?
What does your body feel like?
What does your body look like?
What does your mind feel like?
What actions do you take to tend to your body?
What is your exercise routine?
What are your eating habits?
What actions do you take to tend to your mind?
What, if any, are your health challenges?
   a. How do you handle health challenges?

Why

Why is having good health important to you?
   a. Is living a healthy lifestyle in alignment with your authentic self? If so, how?
   b. Does being healthy support you in expressing yourself fully? If so, how?
   c. Do you love your state of health?
   e. Are you passionate about being healthy? If so, how do you know?

Who

Who does being healthy impact? And how does it impact them?
Who supports you in living a healthy lifestyle?

Where

Where do you take care of yourself?
   a. Do you workout at home, outdoors or at a gym?
   b. Are you in a conducive environment to think clearly?
   c. Are you in a conducive environment for positive thinking?
   d. Describe your environment.
   e. Where do you eat healthy meals?

When

When do you spend time taking care of yourself?
   a. How much time do you spend taking care of yourself?
   b. What is your exercise schedule?
   c. How much time do you spend selecting and preparing your meals?
   d. How much time do you spend clearing your mind and thinking positive thoughts?

Community

* Use this worksheet to describe your **dream** commitment to Community.
* When answering each question be as descriptive as possible.
* Give plenty of examples.

What

What do you do for your community?

Why

Why do you choose to make a difference in your community?
a. Is it in alignment with your authentic self? If so, how?
b. Are you able to express yourself fully? If so, how?
c. Are you passionate about the difference you make in your community? If so, how do you know?
d. Are you using your gifts, talents and skills? If so, how?

Who

Who is impacted by what you do in your community?

Where

Where do you make a difference in your community?

When

When do you spend time making a difference in your community?
a. How often do you do community work?

Education

* Use this worksheet to describe your *dream* Education.
* When answering each question be as descriptive as possible.
* Give plenty of examples.

What

What do you want to learn?
What are your educational goals?
What do you give to your education?
What do you receive from your education?

Why

Why do you want to learn?
  a. How does it feel to learn?
  b. Does it support you in expressing yourself fully?
     If so, how?
  c. Are your gifts, talents and skills growing?
     If so, how?
  d. Are you passionate about learning?
     If so, how do you know?

Who

Who is impacted by your education?
Who supports you in your education?

Where

Where do you get your education?

When

When do you spend time getting your education?
  a. How much time do you spend learning?
  b. How often do you choose to learn?

Did you have any epiphanies? Did you notice where you are in perfect alignment with your authentic self and where you are not? Perhaps, you validated that you are in a career that you love and are passionate about. Maybe you realized that you want to live closer to your family or friends. Did you realize you are right on target with your educational goals? Do you spend the amount of time you want to on your spiritual practices? Perhaps you want a better relationship with your mother. Maybe you want to get involved with a social cause but haven't because you have too many commitments on your plate.

Women tend to have a tough time releasing friends, intimate partners or family members even when they are no good for us. Perhaps you noticed that you are holding on to someone that claims to truly love you, but spends more time making attempts to change you? Or seems to never be satisfied with you? Guess what? It is time to do what it takes to release them from your life. Releasing someone does not always mean pushing them out of your life completely although there are definitely situations that call for that. Rather, it means releasing the emotional attachment you have to them. It is in this way that you ensure you are not led by your feelings in the relationship and are in it because you truly desire to be. In other words, this person is in your life because you choose to have them in your life and for no other reason. There is a saying "If you love someone then let them go, if they come back to you they are yours. If they do not then they were never meant to be."[6] If the person was meant to be in your life they will love, accept and rejoice in your authentic self.

This is where the rubber meets the road. When you identify the differences between your current state of affairs and your true desires, then you take action to shift your circumstances in the direction of your dreams. Again, this is where things can seem difficult but you *must not be afraid to rock the boat if you want to live a life filled with your true desires. You simply get to ground yourself and ensure that your choices are coming from a place of love – the love you have for yourself. You will find that when you operate from a place of self-love, love will spill out into the very situation you are tackling.*

Chapter 10

It's a Bold, Bold World Out There

"I hope you never fear those
mountains in the distance
Never settle for the path of least resistance
Living might mean taking chances
But they're worth taking
Lovin' might be a mistake
But it's worth making"

- I Hope You Dance, A song by Lee Ann Womack

M E A N

I had been in this position before. I did not get along with my
boss but this time was particularly volatile. There seemed to
be more tension than ever before. My boss, Melissa, was a
woman who had an impressive resume and was now a VP at a
major Fortune 500 company. Normally, I would be proud of a
woman who has done so well for herself but we could not even
be in meetings together without challenging each others intel-

lect and power. On top of that, Melissa was not popular around the office. She was a workaholic and made others feel bad for not following suit. Her whole department spoke unkindly of her and they often spoke of how unhappy they were in their jobs because of her rigid rules and micromanagement style.

When I went home at night I would vent and complain to whoever would listen. Interestingly, I would toggle between my feelings about the situation. Sometimes I felt bad for Melissa and sometimes I wanted to tear into her. It was not like me to have such a short temper with people, in fact I considered myself a very loving person so it really bothered me that I was being this way. But for some reason when I got around her I simply could not help but be reactive and combative. It was like I had no control over my behavior when I was around her.

The situation began to be a thorn in my side as I realized I was expending a great deal of energy on it. I desperately wanted to get out from under it. As I reflected more and more on this issue I started to realize that this relationship had power over me. Melissa had the ability to shift my attitude to a point where I was not being myself. I decided to spend some time getting grounded in my true feelings about the situation. Rather than complain to my friends, I chose to take it all within and see what I could discover about myself. I cross-examined myself with a barrage of thought provoking questions. What is it about this woman that bothers me so much? Is there something about her that I don't like about myself? Is there another way I can handle this situation? How can I bring more of me, the loving person I am, into this situation? What do I want out of this relationship with her? When I started to answer these questions, I came to the awareness that I wanted to reach out to Melissa and simply be friends with her. I realized that if Melissa was making people miserable at work, perhaps she was miserable in her personal life.

So I decided to do something that went against every unwritten rule in Corporate America. As crazy as it sounded, I made up my mind that I was going to call the Vice President of my department at her home, apologize for my behavior up to this point and accept responsibility for the condition of our relationship. Then I was going to tell her that I would like to be friends and invite her out to dinner. It felt totally in alignment with my true self so I was confident in my decision. I did not care what people would think and most importantly I did not have any expectations of Melissa's response. Whether Melissa was interested or not in my invitation I wanted to get across that I am there for her and wanted to develop a friendship. I had a great sense of relief. Now all I had to do was carry out my plan. I had to get Melissa's home phone number and catch her at home. I knew that I needed to catch her out of our work environment which would be hard since she was always at the office.

Later that week, I received an email from Melissa letting the department know that she was going to be out for the next two weeks for medical reasons. In the email it also stated that she could be contacted for urgent situations at her home. I could not believe it! It was the perfect opportunity to reach her at home.

I gave her a call but we played a bit of phone tag for the next few days. When we finally connected I was at work in my cubicle. I switched to a conference room to have more privacy. When I started speaking I found myself getting very emotional as I apologized for the nature of our relationship and expressed to Melissa that what I had really wanted all this time was to be friends with her but did not know how to express it. It was not what I had planned to say but it was the truth. I went on to tell her that the reason I was so reactive, and out of control, was because I was going against what I truly desired. I continued by inviting her to dinner sometime. For a moment there was only silence. I suspected that Melissa was trying to figure out how to respond when suddenly I began to hear sobbing. She was crying and it quickly escalated. I let Melissa go through her emotions and waited until she could respond. When she did, she explained to me that she had just been in the other room telling her mother how she has no friends and that her life is comprised of only work which doesn't even bring her joy. She continued to tell me that this call could not have been better timed because she was beginning to give up on being happy. I felt so good about the call! I knew it was a transformative moment for both of us. I realized the power of being me and Melissa now had someone to call a friend.

Our relationship blossomed inside and outside of work. Melissa was finding her joy as our friendship evolved. She was learning how to be herself and stop hiding behind her success at work. She was learning how to access being vulnerable, loving, joyful and courageous. I believed in the good nature of Melissa and felt that as she became a happier person she would turn the entire work environment into a thriving and positive place to be. It happened. Over the next several months, Melissa turned many of her broken relationships on the job into positive ones. She was being her true self, out in the open for all to see and she was no longer hiding it. There were still a few people that had no interest in coming together but at least she tried. Instead of retaliating and handing over her power, she continued to be herself and hoped they would come around.

It wasn't long before Melissa's department became the place to be. It was a great environment on a personal and professional level. It shifted from a place where people were either quitting or transferring out, to a place of interest. Job openings were quickly filled with great candidates and the group meshed as a powerful team.

TIME

*B*y getting in alignment with my authentic self and getting bold about it, I not only made an impact on one person's life but it resonated to an entire department of people! In order to do so, there were some choices I had to make.

I made the choice to take responsibility for the failed relationship and from there I was able to come up with a solution. It was not the only possible solution but it was the one I chose. Remember there are limitless possibilities to the choices we make with every new moment that comes our way. I could have gotten more outrageous by going to her house or I could have been more passive by simply modifying my behavior around her but not necessarily expressing to her I wanted to be friends. The key is that the choice I made was my true desire.

Another distinction is that I looked *within* for a solution to the problem rather than let it be someone else's problem. Let me be clear about this, it is much easier for us to find the "issue" somewhere other than within ourselves. It is our natural 'go to.' The last place we look is within. Meanwhile, it is the most powerful place to start! You see the quicker we can look within the quicker we get connected with our authenticity which will provide honest guidance to a solution. You see it is not placing "blame", it is quite the contrary. It is about creating a shift in the situation regardless of whether there is someone at fault.

I made the choice to let go of my fears about what people would think of me. Often we allow judgment from others to influence our behavior. But what happens when you focus your attention on others with the intention of doing good, you tend not to care so much about what people think. It is no longer about you, it becomes about the person or cause you are serving. And when you remove your personal investment out of the way, you find that you will do whatever it takes to make that difference you set out to create.

I made the choice to detach myself from the result. I got clear on why I wanted to call my boss rather than my expectations of her response. I knew that I wanted to call whether she embraced me or rejected me. While I am glad that she embraced me, I would have been at peace – *at my mean* – either way. I knew from that point forward she would at least know where I stood and that I was on her team. We often get caught up in our results rather than experience and learn from the journey it takes to get there.

I made the choice to put aside my ego! If you remember, I define the ego as the entity of ourselves that protects how we are presented in the world primarily on a superficial level. It was my ego that had me in the power struggle with my boss. My ego was taking great measures to protect my "territory" through the battles. We all have an ego and at times it certainly seems to serve a purpose. As long as we are cognizant of when it is acting on our behalf, we can control it. If not, it can move us in a direction other than that of our authentic self.

Making these choices was authentic for me and resulted in sharing myself boldly in the world. Someone could be in the exact same situation I was and her choices could look totally different based on what is authentic for her. The key is that when you operate authentically, you accept the opportunities to do so powerfully with people whether it looks pretty or ugly. Never shy away from the difference you were put on Earth to do.

LOVE

*L*ove yourself so fully that you share yourself with others. When you are full of self-love, love cannot help but over-flow from you into the world. The love you give will trans-form and make a difference with people. It's a ripple effect. Have you ever been around someone who has such a wonderful aura that it has a positive impact on you? Perhaps it was her joy demonstrated with a beautiful smile or her self-love exud-ing through her as an air of confidence. But something about them just caught your attention and was contagious! I have had a few moments like this in my life but one in particular stands out. It was when I met a woman named Robin Lynn. She was the Trainer of a transformational, life-changing, workshop that I participated in. In my eyes, she was extraordinary. The differ-ence she was able to make with people was amazing and she did it in a way that seemed effortless. She was refreshing simply by being herself and being clear about what she was put on Earth to do. She knew how to *be* loving in many ways. If she had to get tough with folks so that they may have their breakthrough she did so and if she needed to embrace someone so that they felt loved and supported, she did that too. When the training was complete, not only did I know I had been transformed for life but I knew I wanted this woman in my life in some way. I just wanted to be around her so that some of her 'magic' would rub off on me. At times I laugh at my reaction to her because it was like she was a star and I was a fan. But in reality, she was the most authentic person I had ever met and she was living her purpose that was changing thousands of people's lives. At the time, that was a revelation for me.

Chapter 11

There's No Place Like Being Authentic

"Here's where I stand,
Here's who I am
Love me, but don't tell me who I have to be
Here's who I am,
I'm what you see."

- Here's Where I Stand, A song by Tiffany Taylor

M E A N

I had been single for about a year and I was starting to believe marriage was not for me. If relationships in the dating stage were so challenging and at times painful, then marriage just seemed like a permanent uphill battle that I would rather not partake in. However, I knew I wanted to be a mother. I decided that if I did not meet someone that I wanted to have children with by the age of thirty-four I was going to adopt a child. This gave me a solid four years of alone time and that sounded perfect to me.

I was really into doing things by myself. I went for facials, pedicures and massages on a regular basis. Going to dinner and a movie on my own was a common practice. I watched about ten NBA games a week, usually in the evenings, in my pajamas, hair a mess and with a big bowl of salad in lieu of any sort of cooking. I constantly came up with innovative ways to deepen my relationships with friends and family. I also trained for and completed a half-marathon that was a big dream of mine. I was basically choosing to partake in all the things that brought me joy.

One of my latest routines at work was to meet up with my friend in the morning for a healthy breakfast and look at the men that showed interest in her online. My friend was a member of Match.com and we had a blast looking at pictures and reading about men that had expressed their interest in her. Some of the men's profiles were really funny and some looked promising. After a few months of perusing Match.com, I decided that I would like to join my friend as a member so that I could do some light dating. Mostly because I loved to dine out and felt it would be nice to be taken out every now and then. Plus, I found the online dating world intriguing and thought it would be fun to meet some of these people and compare them to their profiles. But I was very clear that I did not want to enter into a committed relationship. Boy did I have fun! I went out with some of the oddest men I had ever met! They were all quite handsome but each of them sure had a story. I even developed nicknames for them.

Let's see, first there was *Stalker Boy*. He decided that he was in love with me after a few phone calls and one stint at Starbucks. As soon as he made me aware of this, I quickly let him know that I was no longer interested in dating him and felt it best that we did not speak anymore so that he could get over me. He had trouble obliging and continued to call for months. There was also *J-Lo boy*. He was a personal trainer with a great body to match. He seemed quite self-involved in our phone discussions but when he asked me out, I accepted his invitation. He took me out to lunch and I quickly found myself in a one-way conversation primarily about how he was going to be on J-Lo's new television show. In fact every conversation from that point forward was about his experience at the J-Lo filming. It got tired very fast. I had to let him know I was no longer interested in him. To no surprise he did not mind at all.

After a while, the dating scene got old so I put my Match.com profile on hold. I noticed in my state of single-ness, that I had gotten more confident in who I am and had really learned to loved myself. The whole dating experience really affirmed that I did not feel the need to have a man in my life and that if I ever entered into a relationship again it would be because I desired to do so.

I had clarity and self-love which I had never experienced in such fullness. I not only transformed my life but I also transformed all my relationships to loving and fulfilled ones.

A couple months went by and life was going great, when I decided to take advantage of the last couple weeks of my Match. com membership. I figured "What the heck, it can't hurt to go on a couple more dates?" It was then that a young, handsome minister took virtual interest in me and sent me a "wink" through the online system. A wink was a way of expressing interest in someone while sending them your online profile so that they can read about you. He peeked my interest. I learned that not only was he a minister but he was also an author, life coach and motivational speaker. That all seemed very cool so I winked back at him. Next he wrote me a wonderful email introducing himself. We corresponded in email for about a week when I let him know that I was going to get off Match.com because it had gotten boring again and that he could email me at my personal email address. He came back with the suggestion that we talk on the phone to see if there was any chemistry between us. That sounded appealing to me since he seemed like a wonderful person. At this point, I did not necessarily think of him as a love interest but something within me really felt this man had come into my life for a bigger reason than I knew at this point.

Our first phone conversation was three hours long. We had so many philosophies in common that there was a lot to talk about. Before the end of the conversation, he wasted no time in asking me out. It was really impressive that he actually looked at my list of favorite places and chose one as our first date location. He got lots of cool points for that! Our first date was amazing. He was dressed in a sharp suit and looked great. His stature was smaller than most of the men I had ever dated, but there was something so huge about him. Almost majestic. We ate a fantastic dinner overlooking the beach. In prior conversations we had both mentioned that we did not get to the beach enough so he suggested that we take a walk along the beach. He made a quick stop at a store before we reached the beach. And once there he spread out a towel for me to sit down on while he without hesitation sat down in the sand. It was romantic and classy of him. We ended up engulfed in each other's every word for the next six hours. We watched the sun come up. But just before then, fireworks went off in the sky! To us it was a sign that this connection was something special.

The next day he was headed to Venezuela for a spiritual retreat and since all my previous Match.com dates got botched, I just knew that this would be where the fairytale ended. So I said goodnight and was prepared to never hear from him again. But this time, while I thought it would be nice to hear from him, I was not going to be thrown off the wonderful path that I was on if he didn't call.

It turned out he called me twice from Venezuela and even sang a sweet song on my voicemail when I was not available to answer his call. Soon after his return we began to date and spend a lot of time together. He had recently gotten out of a long relationship and I felt it would be best to take time to heal from the break up before jumping into a relationship with me. And he did heal. It was such a wonderful dating experience for me. I had never before experienced being with a man that supplemented my life. I never thought I could have it all. I could be my authentic self no matter what. I could do all the things I love to do. I could have strong, healthy relationships with all my loved ones, live my dreams and love fearlessly.

I was choosing to have him in my life for all the right reasons.

Within a year, he asked me to marry him. I said yes. We choose each other every day and brought two amazing girls into the world, Angelina and Kameela.

T I M E

Wow, what a transformation! I had been on a heck of a journey to self-love and acceptance before I got into a successful relationship. *Now hear me, and hear me clearly, by no means am I saying that having an intimate partner in your life is the culmination of loving yourself fully.* I would be the last person to even imply for a moment that a woman needs another person to be perfect, whole and complete. However, for *me* the gap I was operating with for many years of my life, manifested in unhealthy relationships with men, so this story demonstrates my healing. I finally entered into a partnership that was truly supplemental. The key was that I no longer felt in need of it. I was not in search of it. I was not looking for a relationship to fit a purpose in my life. *I was no longer operating with gaps.*

I took the time to learn how I love to be, what I love to do and what I love to have. *And I was making my choices accordingly, resulting in my true desires.* It was imperative that I spent the time getting to know myself and simply being with myself. I was having a blast and did not need anyone around to do so. It was during this time that I became stronger. *I let my authentic self marinate.* I got grounded in who I am to the point where no person, thing or experience had the power to jolt me. When I was encountering all the calamitous dating situations, I was never desperate for one to lead to something more. In fact, I found the humor in it all. Humor is one of my values. I love to laugh and make people laugh. Not only does it feel good, I believe it has a healing effect. *This is a demonstration of how the core of who you are shines through when you are devoted to being your authentic self.*

One day, unbeknownst to me, I was open to this loving relationship. It came naturally. I could see him for who he was rather than what he could provide. I could enjoy and appreciate every moment I shared with him rather than preoccupy myself with drama, fear and worry. I could be myself under all circumstances without crumbling if he did not like what he saw. I could feel great about myself whether he was around or not. I could be optimistic about a future with a man rather than reference my past and believe it will never work. *Such clarity came from operating at my mean – that place of authenticity, relentless self-love and confident self-acceptance.*

I was no longer of the mindset that my past relationships were a forecast for my future ones. I was no longer collecting evidence from my past that my relationships could never be healthy. I had released my past. I had forgiven myself for choosing such relationships. I was over it. My past no longer had power over me. I was able to look at each new moment with a fresh set of eyes. *I appreciated each new moment for what it was – an opportunity to express my authentic self.*

Soon after I got married, I changed careers from engineering to writer, life coach and trainer serving women all over the world. *I am sharing my authentic self boldly which has opened the doors to living my God-given purpose.* There are times I come out of one of my workshops and say to myself "Wow, did I just create that?" "Did I just help transform those women's lives?" And I can proudly say yes, because I know this is mine to do.

LOVE

I put the following quote at the bottom of every graduation certificate I give out to my workshop participants upon completion, *"It is when you look within that you realize you have everything you need to create all that you desire."* No matter what life throws your way may you never lose sight of this truth. You've got it all! You have the power to realize all of your true desires. When in doubt, think of me, I'm living proof.

I love you.

ENDNOTES

1. National Institute of Justice & Centers for Disease Control & Prevention (1998). *Prevalence, Incidence and Consequences of Violence Against Women Survey.* Retrieved from http://www.ojp.usdoj.gov/nij/pubs-sum/172837.htm

2. World Health Organization (2001). Retrieved from http://www.who.int/mip2001/files/2269/239-ViolenceAgainstWomenforMIP.pdf

3. Bulimia Nervousa Health Center (2011). Retrieved from http://www.webmd.com

4. *"Reviving Ophelia: Saving the Selves of Adolescent Girls"*, Pipher, Mary, Ph.D., 1994

5. Nelson, Colin (2006) *"One-Third of Girls in the U.S. Are Sexually Active by Age 15, CDC Says"* Clinical Psychiatry News Article. (Vol. 34, Issue 6, Page 35) Retrieved from http://www.clinicalpsychiatrynews.com

6. Anonymous

Anita Maria Loren Ross presents

Deeper Kind of Love

An Experience for Women

Are you a woman in a relationship that
you know isn't working for you?

Are you a woman struggling to have your voice heard?

Are you a woman who spends more time
taking care of others than yourself?

Are you a woman who spends more money on
clothes than you can afford?

Are you a woman who eats too much or
who does not eat enough?

Are you a woman who is too busy
to spend a moment alone?

If you answered yes to one or more of these questions,
you want to attend Anita Ross' Workshop:

"A Deeper Kind of Love: An Experience for Women"

The workshop where women come to get off of the emotional, self-esteem roller coaster and sky rocket their self-worth – GUARANTEED!

In this powerful experiential workshop you will uncover the true feelings you have about yourself and how they directly impact the trajectory of your life. Spend some time learning to listen to your heart, discover your authentic self, explore your true voice and experience loving yourself fully. We will learn, laugh, share stories, reflect, and even shed a tear or two, in a relaxed, safe environment, where you can let your hair down and just be free!

For workshop schedule or booking information,
please visit us at: **www.anitaross.net**

TEEN DREAM CAMP
" Where dreams are born where dreamers shine! "

Together with her husband, Kevin Ross, Anita is also doing powerful work with teenagers through their 501(c)3 non-profit organization, Teen Dream Camp.

Teen Dream Camp starts teens down a positive path toward identifying with their uniqueness, tapping into the dreams in their hearts, establishing a winning attitude and learning how to use the time-tested methods for success and achievement.

For camp information, to get involved or to make a donation, please visit us at: **www.teendreamcamp.org**